DEDICATION

This book is dedicated to all who seek to protect the wilderness and especially to my children, Cheryl Anne, Miles, and Jason, who share my love for the out-of-doors.

Aloha!

Hiking Maui
The Valley Isle

by Robert Smith

A Hawaiian Outdoor Adventures Publication

FIRST EDITION July 1975
Second printing September 1976
SECOND EDITION September 1977
Second printing April 1978
THIRD EDITION December 1979
Second printing February 1982
FOURTH EDITION January 1984
Second printing January 1985
Third printing June 1986
FIFTH EDITION June 1989
Second printing January 1991
SIXTH EDITION July 1993
Second printing June 1995
SEVENTH EDITION April 1997
Second printing /update May 1999

Maps by Kevin G. Chard
Layout by N. Karakawa
Cover photo by Diane G. Harper
Photos by the author and Diane G. Harper

Library of Congress Card Catalog Number
International Standard Book Number 0-924308-06-0
Manufactured in the United States
Published by
    Hawaiian Outdoor Adventures Publications

ACKNOWLEDGEMENTS

Many people made significant contributions to this book. Ruth Wryn and Vi Saffery of the Wailuku Public Library and Gail Bartholomew, librarian at Maui Community College, labored in good humor over my numerous requests and offered some advice. Forester, Robert Hobdy with the Hawaii State Department of Natural Resources, generously shared his experiences and expertise gathered in walking almost every foot of the Valley Isle. Mike Baker, Trail Specialist with DLNR, responded to my numerous queries with valuable information. Haleakala National Park staff members read and offered helpful suggestions for which I am grateful. Thanks to Fred Samia who assisted by reading the manuscript and correcting my goofs. I am indebted to Diane G. Harper who contributed some of the photos included in this book and who assisted me on many of the trails. A special mahalo to Nancy Smith and to Cheryl Smith-Litchie for their companionship on many of the hikes and for their endurance in typing the manuscript for this book.

Robert Smith
Kula, Maui, Hawaii

Books by Robert Smith

Hawaii's Best Hiking Trails

Hiking Maui, the Valley Isle

Hiking Oahu, the Capital Isle

Hiking Hawaii, the Big Island

Hiking Kauai, the Garden Isle

Video by Robert Smith

Hawaii on Foot

CAUTION–WARNING–CAUTION

On Sunday, May 9, 1999 tragedy struck at the base of the waterfall in Sacred Falls State Park on Oahu. A landslide from the near-vertical walls of the valley sent tons of boulders, rocks and dirt onto unsuspecting hikers. Eight persons were killed and dozens injured.

Although thousands of people annually hike throughout the Aloha State without mishap or injury, active outdoorspeople should be aware that landslides in Hawaii are common. Hawaii's strata is extremely brittle and unstable and affected by rain and by periods of drought. Rain can undermine the dirt supporting rocks and boulders and drought can cause the dirt to shrink. During periods of heavy rainfall, flash flooding is common.

Be alert and cautious when hiking particularly in narrow valleys, on ridges and along steep, precipitous cliffs.

The State Department of Land and Natural Resources and private landowners may close access to a trail temporarily or permanently so please respect posted warnings. Failure to do so can result in criminal prosecution.

PLEASE respect "KAPU" ("NO TRESPASSING") signs.

CONTENTS

(HIKING MAP - NEXT PAGE)

MAUI—HIKING

CENTRAL ZONE

WEST ZONE

EAST ZONE

HALEAKALA ZONE

SOUTH ZONE

NAKALELE LIGHTHOUSE
BLOWHOLE
KAHAKULOA
WAIHEE
HONOKAHUA
NAPILI
KAANAPALI
IAO NEEDLE 2,250 FT
PUU KUKUI 5,788 FT
KAHULUI AIRPORT
WAILUKU
LAHAINA
LAUNIUPOKO STATE PK
OLOWALU
LAHAINA PALI
MAALAEA
PUUNENE
PUKALANI
KEALIA POND
KIHEI
KALAMA PK
MAKENA
PUU OLAI
LA PEROUSE BAY
KAMANAMANA POINT
HUAKINI BAY
KAUPO
NUU
KIPAHULU
ULUPALAKUA
POLIPOLI PK
KULA
PIIHOLO
WAIHOU SPRINGS
PAIA
BALDWIN PK
HOOKIPA BEACH
WAIKAMOI RIDGE
KEANAE
BLUE POOL
HANA
WAIANAPANAPA STATE PK
HELIO'S GRAVE
HALEAKALA NATIONAL PK KIPAHULU SECTION
WAIMOKU FALLS
HALEAKALA NATIONAL PK 10,023 FT
SKYLINE TR

HIGHWAYS ⊙
HIKES □
UNPAVED ROADS ------
(MAP NOT TO SCALE)

N E W S

PART I:

INTRODUCTION

Wailua Falls

"MAUI NO KA OI"

Adventurers come in all shapes, sizes and dispositions. Some enjoy the challenge of trudging through a quagmire in wind and rain in order to stand atop a mountain whose name is unknown to most people. Others find wonder in a volcano conformed like the surface of the moon, with no familiar sights or sounds except the sounds made by the wind. Still others prefer a leisurely walk to a fern-rimmed pool and a cool swim beneath a waterfall.

All these options are possible within 729 square miles in a land of contrasts, in a land of unmatched beauty, in a land often equated with paradise by the casual visitor as well as the native-born. It's the Valley Isle - Maui. As the familiar stenciled T-shirt proclaims, "Maui No Ka Oi" - "Maui is the best." Maui has 150 miles of coastline, with 33 miles suitable for swimming. The Valley Isle possesses more beach area than any other Hawaiian island, which probably accounts for its exceptional popularity.

The island of Maui is the result of eruptions of two large volcanoes, which first formed separate land masses that were later joined by succeeding eruptions. Although some debate exists over the origin of the name, many people believe the island was named after Maui, a legendary superman, who lassoed the sun to bring daylight to the island. In spite of this male giant's influence, locals refer to Maui as "our beautiful lady" because of the island's curvaceous physical appearance. Topped by 10,023-foot Haleakala, the lady's skirt fans out in multitudinous pleats in the form of valleys and gulches. Some are usually dry, awaiting the seasonal rains. Others are usually wet and abound with introduced and native flora and fauna.

Maui is not only the second largest of the Hawaiian Islands in size (Hawaii is the largest) but also the second most visited. More and more tourists are departing from the tour-bus route and becoming familiar with a Maui previously known only to natives. Campers, bicyclists and hikers are now more numerous and visible. There are hikes on Maui to satisfy the tenderfoot as well as the backpacker: short, easy hikes for the family, which reveal the beauty of the valleys, and more strenuous hikes, which do not necessarily reveal more but which fulfill the spirit of the more adventurous.

This guide outlines short, easy hikes to suit the short-term visitor, and longer, more ambitious hikes for the visitor with more time and energy to expend. The hiker becomes familiar with a different Maui and views this beautiful lady from a perspective unknown to the ordinary tourist. It is with mixed feelings that I reveal her secrets, for the result may be an intrusion on heretofore pristine areas. Some parts of the island have not yet felt the impact of the visitor, with his frequently careless habits and the resulting pollution and abuse. I proceed under the assumption that the hiker is of a special breed: one who loves and cares for the land, one who tends to minimize his impact on the land, and one who does not violate the earth without feeling he has violated himself.

Hana Bay

THE FIVE ZONES OF MAUI

For convenience, I have divided Maui into five zones. Each zone has its own unique character, yet shares certain features with the other sections. The view that "if you have seen one valley, you have seen them all" does not apply to Maui. Differences can be attributed in large part to annual rainfall, which varies from a trifle to over 400 inches; to man-made alterations made in connection with irrigation systems; and to introduced flora and fauna which have presented problems for native species. Since the terrain and the climate are so varied, hiking is all the more exciting and pleasurable.

EAST ZONE
The 50-mile road from Kahului to Hana, in the East Zone, is regarded by many visitors and locals as the most extraordinarily beautiful 50-mile drive in the world. While natives complain and tourists sit entranced, the Hana Highway continues on its bumpy, twisting, narrow, exquis-

ite course. Reportedly there are some 900 curves on this road that winds a twisting path through valleys and gulches profusely ornamented by nature. Don't bother to count; everyone comes up with a different total. But do drive slowly if you are unfamiliar with this road. Minimum driving time is two hours one-way.

The East Zone encompasses the Paia-Kaenae-Hana townships as well as the popular Kipahulu section of Haleakala National Park. Many tourist maps identify this latter area as the "Seven Sacred Pools." There are, however, more than seven pools, and there is nothing sacred about the area. Native forests, black-sand beaches and a lot of old Hawaii are available to the visitor here. Although the hiker is annoyed by rain and mosquitoes, the East Zone contains some of the best hiking trails and hiking accommodations on the island. Waterfalls abound, and hikers delight in swimming in the generous pools formed by the falling water.

The road from Hana to the Kipahulu section of Haleakala National Park is more narrow than the first 50 miles of the Hana Highway. The road is passable, but drive slowly and watch for oncoming cars. The road beyond the pools is mostly unpaved, rocky, bumpy and poorly maintained, with many holes. It is not advisable to drive there in an ordinary passenger or rental car. Query Park Rangers regarding road conditions around the south side.

HALEAKALA ZONE

The "Upcountry" or Haleakala Zone includes the Haleakala-Kula-Polipoli portions of Maui. Hiking is particularly enjoyable in this mountain zone because of the broad panoramas of the island and, indeed, on clear days, views of the neighboring islands of Kahoolawe, Molokini, Lanai, Molokai and Hawaii. It is also the home of the rare silversword plant, which delights both tourists and residents and the equally rare Hawaii State bird -- the Nene.

Hiking in Haleakala National Park is an experience not soon forgotten. Hiking year-round is possible. Rental cabins and campgrounds are available there. Thirty miles of trails crisscross the Park with sights to stimulate the senses and to calm the spirit.

For those seeking solitude, Polipoli State Park is an outstanding hiking and camping area for the whole family. Several short easy hiking trails snake under a canopy of giant trees most of which were introduced to Maui as part of a reforestation program. Mountain bikers and horses share the area, so be alert when hiking the trails. It's a marvelous full-day experience particularly when it includes an overnight stay in the State rental cabin or in a tent in the campground. This allows you to explore the Park more extensively and leisurely.

SOUTH ZONE

The towns of Kihei and Makena and the Wailea resort complex with its championship golf courses are in the South Zone. Without doubt, the south shore has the finest swimming beaches on the island, as well as areas for the popular sports of snorkeling and fishing at Kamaole and Makena.

Hiking in the South Zone is limited to the fine coastal area there and to the most recent lava flow on the island, which occurred sometime around 1750. A walk through the Kealia Pond National Wildlife Refuge affords an opportunity to see several rare and endangered birds and, with luck, the endangered hawksbill turtle. This region rivals the Lahaina area in temperature, rainfall and sunny days.

CENTRAL ZONE

In the business center of the island, the Central Zone, are the towns of Kahului and Wailuku, the latter serving as the county seat. With the recent construction of two major shopping centers within a mile of each other, Kahului has surpassed Wailuku in their respective efforts to attract shoppers.

The major hiking area in the Central Zone is Iao Valley,which contains numerous streams and swimming holes and walks through a densely foliated "jungle" frequented by both residents and visitors. The Iao Needle is a richly foliated pin-

nacle which seems to have been forced up
through the valley floor to a height of 1,200 feet.
It is a popular tourist attraction.

Waihee Valley and Waihee Ridge are two marvelous hikes a few miles north of Kahului. The
former trek follows a stream into a heavily vegetated valley to a generous swimming hole, and
the latter hiking trail follows a ridge line above
the valley floor to several vista points that offer
outstanding views of the northeast side and beyond to Haleakala.

WEST ZONE

The West Zone encompasses the popular tourist center of Lahaina-Kaanapali-Napili and accommodates the bulk of the tourist population.
Lahaina was not only the first capital of the
Islands but also a 19th-century whaling port of
considerable reputation. The town abounds in
memorabilia of this romantic period.

The Lahaina Pali Trail, originally constructed
in 1840, was surveyed, cleared and brushed in
1992 and reopened. This historic trail parallels
the southwest coast above the ocean where, between November and March, migratory humpback whales can be spotted in the waters below.

More history is revealed at the Olowalu
Petroglyphs, some of the best examples of ancient Hawaiian art on the islands and at the
David Malo gravesite above the Lahaina "L" a
thousand feet above Lahaina.

SAFE HIKING ON MAUI

In 1989, the state Department of Health issued a warning to campers and hikers that portable water filters will not protect them from the dangerous bacterium leptospirosis. Health officials say that only boiling or chemical treatment will control this disease that is found in surface water throughout Hawaii. It enters the body through breaks in the skin or through mucous membranes and can cause flu-like symptoms. The disease can also be fatal.

Portable water filters may protect against giardia, salmonella and other bacteria and parasites, but not leptospirosis. The department's release stated that vigorous boiling is the only reliable method of purification. Tablets containing hydroperiodide will work if boiling is not possible, according to health authorities.

Maui is a relatively safe island to hike and camp. Nevertheless, you should take precautions as you would on the mainland. The fact is that much of the violence directed against hikers and

campers is drug related. If a person is looking
for drugs then he is looking for trouble. You are
cautioned never to hike or camp alone. As a general rule, the farther you hike and camp away
from populated areas, the safer your experience
is likely to be. NEVER leave valuables unpro-
tected. I always carry a daypack containing those
items which I cannot afford to lose -- wallet, air-
line ticket, camera -- and I carry it everywhere.
Yes, even there!

One problem facing the hiker on Maui is the
lack of trailhead signs and trail markers. Most
of the trails contained in this book are well-
defined, but many are not marked. Although I
provide detailed directions to the trailhead and
a trail narrative that makes the trail easy to follow, seasonal rains, floods, and other natural
forces impact on the land to alter it, sometime
significantly. Additionally, trail markers are
sometimes destroyed or removed, I suspect, by
locals who are either mischievous or who wish
to discourage visitors to their favorite places.
Recently, Na Ala Hele, the state-wide trails and
access system, has posted many trailheads and
signage on the trail. Good judgment and a regard for the time-tested rules of hiking are good
protection.

Hikers and campers are always relieved to
learn that there are no poisonous snakes nor is
there any poison ivy and poison oak in Hawaii.
Poisonous centipedes and scorpions are found at

low elevations. The two biggest pests in Hawaii are the mosquito and the cockroach. While neither is fatal to man, both are troublesome. They can make an outdoor experience disagreeable unless precautions are taken. You will have to live with the cockroach, but all the mosquito lotions and sprays seem to provide effective protection. Due to the wet climate, be prepared to make frequent applications.

Unfortunately, some hikers have lost their lives or have been injured because they have violated time-tested safety rules. Remember,

1. DO NOT hike alone.
2. Leave your itinerary and expected time of return with a responsible person. Contact them when you return.
3. Carry a well-stocked first-aid kit.
4. DO NOT hike off the trail. Numerous accidents and deaths have occured when persons have strayed from the trail.
5. Wear bright clothing.
6. Carry a flashlight, matches, mirror, whistle and a cell phone, if available.
7. Many Hawaiian trails are wet and slippery, and the terrain is loose and brittle. Wear hiking boots or strong shoes.
8. Contrary to popular belief, it is not possible to live off the land. Carry your own food.

9.   Although some fruits are available,
     never eat or taste unknown
     fruits or plants.
10. Carry your own water or
    boil or water from streams.
11. A tent with a rain fly ensures
    comfortable and dry nights.
12. Firewood in most places is not
    available or is too wet for use.
    Carry a stove for cooking.
13. Darkness sets in right after sunset.
14. If lost, find an open area and stay put.

To protect the environment, remember,
1.   Clean boots of dirt and seeds
     before hiking.
2.   Carry your own trash out.
3.   Bury personal waste away from streams.
4.   Do washing at least 100 feet away
     from natural water supply.
5.   Respect endangered species.
     DO NOT feed wild animals.

MAUI'S CAMPGROUNDS

Camping on Maui will add a dimension to your visit. Campgrounds range from adequate to good and contain most of the amenities. Fees for state and county campgrounds are modest and camping in Haleakala National Park is free. Consult the camping map for the location of the county, state and national campgrounds, camping shelters, and rental housekeeping cabins. Campers are advised to bring their own equipment because there are no reliable rental companies on Maui.

County Campgrounds

Kanaha Beach Park is on the coast in Central Maui north of the airport.It is the only county campground on Maui. A permit is required and is limited to 15 days per year with a three night maximum. Camping fees are $3.00 for adults and $.50 for persons under 18. The park has outdoor showers, drinking water, tables, and restrooms. For reservations and information, write to the Maui Department of Parks and Recreation. (See Appendix).

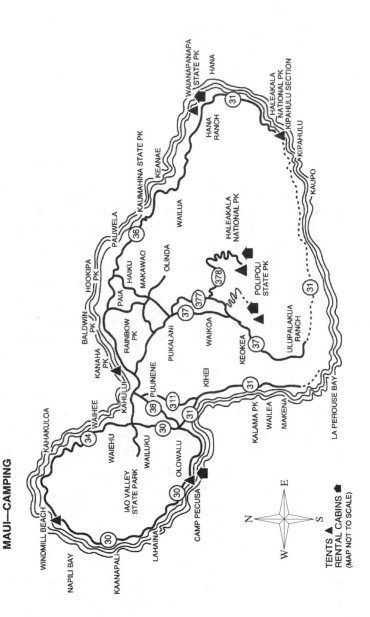

MAUI—CAMPING

WINDMILL BEACH

NAPILI BAY

KAANAPALI

LAHAINA

KAHAKULOA

WAIEHU

WAIHEE

WAILUKU

IAO VALLEY STATE PARK

OLOWALU

CAMP PECUSA

KAHULUI

PUUNENE

KIHEI

KALAMA PK

WAILEA

MAKENA

LA PEROUSE BAY

PUKALANI

RAINBOW PK

KANAHA PK

BALDWIN PK

HOOKIPA PK

PAIA

HAIKU

MAKAWAO

OLINDA

WAIKOA

KEOKEA

ULUPALAKUA RANCH

POLIPOLI STATE PK

HALEAKALA NATIONAL PK

PAUWELA

KAUMAHINA STATE PK

WAILUA

KEANAE

HANA RANCH

WAIANAPANAPA STATE PK

HANA

HALEAKALA NATIONAL PK KIPAHULU SECTION

KIPAHULU

KAUPO

N
E
S
W

TENTS ▲
RENTAL CABINS ◄
(MAP NOT TO SCALE)

State Campgrounds

The State of Hawaii provides two campgrounds on Maui. One is located on the shoreline near Hana and the second in a forest high on the slopes of Haleakala Volcano. Waianapanapa State Park, three miles north of Hana, is on a bluff overlooking a black-sand beach. If you are looking for solitude, the other state campground, at Polipoli State Park, will satisfy you. Polipoli is 31 miles from Wailuku in Maui's upcountry at 6,200 feet in a dense forest is not frequently visited. The maximum length of stay is 5 nights. A fee of $5 per person, per night at all state campgounds (statewide) is expected to go into effect in the summer of 1999. A permit is required from the State Parks office. (See Appendix).

Haleakala National Park Campgounds

The National Park Service operates four campgrounds in Haleakala National Park. One campground is located at Hosmer Grove, a short walk from park headquarters at 7,000 feet. No permit is required. Two wilderness campgrounds are located in the volcano - at Paliku Cabin on the east side and at Holua Cabin on the north side. Tenting is limited to three nights and four days (two nights at one site). Tenting is further limited to 50 persons per day, with 25 persons per camping site. Wilderness

permits are required and available at park
headquarters on a first-come, first-served basis.
Another campground is located at sea level in
the Kipahulu Section of the Park. It is a prim-
itive camping area without water. No permit is
required at Kipahulu. There is no fee for any of
the campgrounds.

Don't pass up hiking and camping in
Haleakala National Park. It is one of the best
places for both in the Islands. (See Appendix).

Private Campgrounds

Two private campgrounds are available on
the westside of the island. The Maui Land &
Pineapple Company allows camping by permission (tel. 669-6201) on their property at Windmill Beach, which is 16 miles north of Lahaina.
Windmill is a good swimming and snorkeling
beach, but there is no water and no facilities.
Camping is $5 per person, per night (See Appen-
dix).

Camp Pecusa is an Episcopal Church Camp
located on the beach near Olowalu, 7 miles
southeast of Lahaina and 14 miles southwest of
Wailuku. A small sign identifies the highway
turnoff. Camping is on a first-come, first-served
basis at a rate of $5 per person, per night. The
camp has an outdoor, solar heated shower,
chemical toilets, picnic tables and campfire pits.
Reservations and information are available (See
Appendix).

A SPECIAL NOTE: Camping has always been an enjoyable and inexpensive way to experience the islands. Recently, however, some campers have been beaten and a few killed. Most of the beatings have been committed by local men, according to the victims. Most of the assaults have taken place at campgrounds that were close to cities or towns where locals congregate. There has been little violence in remote and wilderness areas of the national parks. The best advice is to avoid contact with groups of people.

Camping - Camp Pecusa

MAUI'S HOUSEKEEPING CABINS

In addition to the campgrounds, the State of Hawaii and Haleakala National Park operate comfortable and inexpensive rental housekeeping cabins.

State Rental Cabins
Each of the 12 cabins at Waianapanapa State Park, three miles north of Hana accommodates up to six people and is completely furnished with bedding, towels, cooking and eating utensils, electricity, hot water, showers, electric stoves and refrigerators. The fee schedule at Waianapanapa is $45 for 1-4 persons and $5 for each additional person with a maximum of six in each cabin.

The Polipoli cabin has similar facilities except that it has no electricity and has a gas stove and a cold shower only. The Polipoli cabin accommodates up to 10 persons. Fees for cabin use are $45 for 1-4 persons and $5 for each additional person up to 10. For reservations or permits for cabins, write or contact the Division State Parks. (See Appendix).

Haleakala National Park Rental Cabins

Use of the cabins in Haleakala National Park presents a definite problem because of their popularity with visitors and locals. There are three cabins available in the wilderness -- at Paliku, at Holua and at Kapalaoa (see Haleakala map). Each cabin is equipped with water that must be treated, pit toilet, wood-burning cook stove, firewood, cooking and eating utensils, 12 bunks and mattresses (blankets, pillow and sheets are not supplied). You must bring a warm sleeping bag and propane, although wood is available for cooking and heating. Use is limited to three nights - two nights at any one site. Rates are $40 per night for 1-6 persons and $80 per night for 7-12 persons. Fees include cabin rental and firewood. Cabins have small propane stoves to use for cooking and heating in order to save on firewood.

A lottery is conducted to determine cabin users. To participate, you must write to the Superintendent, Haleakala National Park, at least 60 days in advance forwarding an outline of your proposed trip, including the number in your group, the exact dates and which cabin you want to use each night. You will be contacted only if your request is drawn (See Appendix).

Private Rental Cabins

Cabin facilities are also available at Camp Pecusa for rent by organized groups. Six A-frame

cabins with six cots each, a fully equipped
kitchen and dining hall, and bathrooms with hot
showers are provided at a cost of $9 per person,
per night ($240 minimum charge). Users must
provide their own bedding (four inch foam mattresses are included), transportation, and food.

Driving directions from Kahului to -

H.A. Baldwin Beach Park Campground
(10 miles) Drive east on Route 36 Hana (Highway) to park on left side of the road before Paia
Town.

Kanaha Beach Park Campground
(2 miles) Drive east on Route 32 past Maui Mall,
turn left on Route 361 (Hobron Ave) and turn
right on Amala Place to park on left side of the
road.

**Waianapanapa State Park
Campground & Cabins**
(50 miles) Drive east on Route 36 (Hana
Highway). Before Hana Town, turn left into the
park.

Polipoli State Park Campground & Cabin
(31 miles) Drive east on Route 36, turn right on
Route 37 and drive through Kula section of Maui.
Turn left on Route 377 for 0.4 mile, turn right on
Waipoli Road to park.

Haleakala National Park
Campgrounds - Kipahulu Section

(63 miles) Drive east on Route 36 (Hana High-way). Continue on Route 31 through Hana to the Park.

Halcakala National Park Campgrounds
& Cabins - Wilderness Section (volcano)

(40 miles) Drive east on Route 36, turn right on Route 37, turn left on Route 377 and turn left on Route 378 to Park Headquarters and secure camping permits and/or cabin keys, etc. Drive 11 miles to the summit and trailhead. (Cabins in wilderness only)

Hosmer Grove

(28 miles) Drive east on Route 36, turn right on Route 37, turn   left on Route 377 and turn left on Route 378 to Park entrance. Just inside the Park, turn left to Hosmer Grove.

Camp Pecusa Campground & Cabins

(14 miles) Drive south on Route 38, turn left on Route 30 to Camp on left side of the road just before reaching Olowalu.

Windmill Beach (37 miles) Secure a map to beach when you pickup permit from Maui Land & Pine Co. Drive south on Route 38, turn left on Route 30 through Lahaina and Kapalua to beach.

FOOD AND EQUIPMENT

Although food is more expensive on Maui than on the mainland, it is readily available in the towns. You may visit a local delicatessen that prepares box lunches containing local favorites such as tempura, sweet-and-sour spare ribs and sushi. When fruits are not available along the trail, be certain to visit a local market or roadside stand for mango, papaya, pineapple, passion fruit, and local avocado which comes in the large economy size.

DAYHIKE CHECKLIST
Daypack
Hiking boots or tennis shoes
Plastic water bottle,
    quart size (one per person)
Swiss Army knife
Insect repellent
Shorts
Bathing suit
Sunscreen and tanning lotion

Sunglasses
Whistle for each child
Camera and film
Hat or sun visor
Poncho or raingear
Towel
Waterproof matches
Flashlight
Cell telephone
Hiking Maui

Planning and preparation are particularly important for the backpacker. The following equipment is recommended for overnight hikes and for campers.

BACKPACK CHECKLIST

General Equipment
Frame and pack
Lightweight sleeping bag or blanket
    (heavy bag above 4,000 feet)
Backpack tent with rainfly
Plastic ground cover
Sleep pad
Plastic water bottle, quart size
Swiss Army knife
Flashlight (it helps to explore lava tubes)
40 feet of nylon cord
First-aid kit

Cooking Gear
Backpack stove Fuel
Cooking pots
Fork and spoon
Plastic bowl Sierra cup
Waterproof matches

Clothing
Poncho or raingear
Pants Shorts and/or bathing suit
Hat or Bandana
Undershorts
T-shirts
Socks
Hiking boots

Toilet Articles
Soap (biodegradable)
Toothbrush/powder-paste
Part-roll toilet paper
Chapstick
Comb
Towel
Insect repellent
Sunscreen and tanning lotion
Mirror

Miscellaneous
Sun glasses
Camera and film
Plastic bags
Fishing gear

HAWAIIAN MADE EASY

For your interest, throughout the text wherever a Hawaiian place name is used, I have provided a literal translation if possible. In many instances, Hawaiian names have multiple meanings and even the experts sometimes disagree over the literal meaning. The meanings given here are based on the best information available and on the context in which the name is used. As students of the environment, the Hawaiians had a flair for finding the most expressive words to describe their physical surroundings.

Most visitors are reluctant to try to pronounce Hawaiian words. But with a little practice and a knowledge of some simple rules, you can develop some language skill and add to your Hawaiian experience. Linguists regard Hawaiian as one of the most fluid and melodious languages of the world. There are only twelve letters in the Hawaiian alphabet: five vowels, a, e, i, o, u, and seven consonants, h, k, l, m, n, p, w. Hawaiian is spelled phonetically. Correct pronunciation is

easy if you do not try to force English pronunciation onto the Hawaiian language. Vowel sounds
are simple: a=ah; e=eh; i=ee; o=oh; and u=oo.
Consonant sounds are the same as in English
with the exception of w. The w rule is not ad-
hered to with any consistency by local people.
Generally, w is pronounced "w" at the beginning
of a word and after a. For example, Waimea is
pronounced "Wai-may-ah" and wala-wala is
"wah-lah-wah-lah." Hawaiians usually pronounce w as "w" when it follows o or u: auwaha
is "ah-oo-wah-hah," and hoowali is "hoh-oh-wah-
lee." When w is next to the final letter of a word,
it is variably pronounced "w" and "v"; Wahiawa
is "wah-he-ah-wa," but Hawi is "ha-vee." Listen
to the locals for their treatment of this sound.
Since the Hawaiian language is not strongly ac-
cented, the visitor will probably be understood
without employing any accent.

Some common Hawaiian words:

'aina	land
ali'i	royalty; chief
aloha	welcome; love; farewell
aloha nui loa	much love
hale	house
haole	foreigner; Caucasian
hapa haole	part Caucasian and part ?
heiau	pre-Christian place of worship
hukilau	net pull
kahili	royal feather standard

kahuna	priest
kai	sea
kama'aina	native-born
kane	male
kapu	keep out
kaukau	food
keiki	child
kokua	help
lua	toilet
mahalo	thanks
makai	toward the sea
malihini	newcomer
mele	song
ohana	family
'ono	delicious
'opu	belly
pali	cliff
paniolo	Hawaiian cowboy
pau	finished
puka	hole
pupus	snacks
wahine	female
wikiwiki	hurry up

Some common Pidgin words

brah	brother, as a term of endearment
da kine	whatchamacallit
hana hau	encore
howzit?	what's happening?
shaka!	great! suck 'em up, drink up
talk stink	use profane words
to da max	all the way

USING THIS BOOK

In planning a hike, the reader is advised to consult the Hiking Chart below in order to give due consideration to driving time, hiking time, and the clothing and supplies necessary. I have rated all the hikes and placed them in four categories. A family rated hike is for those who are looking for short, easy hikes. The hardy family classification requires a degree of effort and sound physical condition. Both the strenuous and the difficult hikes require a measure of endurance, since they are longer hikes and most of them involve a considerable gain in altitude. They also require good footwear and more equipment.

Obviously, hiking time varies from person to person, depending on such factors as pace and the extent to which one chooses to linger for lunch and to swim where pools exist. The time noted in the Hiking Chart is based on a leisurely pace. Trail distance is based either on an exact measurement or on an approximation with the aid of a topographic map.

Driving time and mileage cited are based on the posted speed limit and are measured both from the county seat of Wailuku and from Lahaina. Specific driving instructions are provided preceding each hike description.

The equipment noted on the Hiking Chart is minimal for hiking. As a rule, however, I always carry water, food and a first-aid kit. Although the choice between tennis shoes and hiking boots is listed in some cases as optional, I prefer hiking boots in most cases. Obviously, your feet are an important consideration in hiking since it is common, on an island that has experienced extensive volcanic activity, to have volcanic ash or rock underfoot. Usually, shorts or long pants are optional, except in those cases where the brush is thick or when the weather requires warmer clothing.

Drinking water is available from streams in many areas, but it should be boiled or treated since cattle, pigs and goats usually share the water supply. To avoid the chance of illness, carry at least one quart of water per person. In many cases, firewood is at a premium. A small, light, reliable backpacking stove is a convenience and a comfort if you plan to cook out.

Before each hike description you will find the zone, hike rating, trail features, hiking distance and time, specific driving instructions, and introductory notes. On some hikes it is necessary to walk on private property. Information and addresses are provided so that you can secure permission in advance. Permission is usually readily granted either over the telephone or in person when you sign a liability waiver.

In the trail narrative I usually mention the flora and fauna to be seen along the way, especially the unusual and the unique, in an effort to add to your hiking enjoyment. But I don't mention everything, and you may wish to buy one of several guides to plants and animals of the islands, available at many local stores. I recommend *Hawaii's Birds* published by the Hawaii Audubon Society and Angela Kay Kepler's *Maui's Floral Splendor*.

Preceding each trail narrative is a map to help you find the trailhead and to locate trail highlights. The maps show many features of the hikes as well as camping information. The maps are not to scale.

Please respect "kapu" ("No Trespassing") signs. Every effort is made to provide our readers with information when permission is required to hike on private land. Some private landowners allow hiking without their permission and then change their mind, or they withdraw permission without notice.

Waimoku Falls

Hiking Chart: TRAILS

Hiking Area No.	Trail	Family	Hardy Family	Difficult	Strenuous	Distance (miles)	Time (hours)	Gain (feet)	Lahaina Miles	Lahaina Time (hours)	Wailuku Miles	Wailuku Time (hours)	Equipment (Take Food, Carry Water, Walking Shoes, Boots, Rain Gear)	Features (Swimming, Waterfalls, Views, Historical Sites, Fruits)
	EAST ZONE													
1	Waikamoi Ridge	X				1	1½	300	46	1½	27	1	X X	X X
2	Keanae Arboretum	X				2.3	1½	200	53	2	34	1½	X X X X X	X X
3	Keanae Village	X				1	½		53	2	34	1½	X	X X
4	Blue Pool		X			1.4	1		69	3	50	2	X X X X	X X X X X
5	Waianapanapa	X							70	3	51	2½	X X X X	X X X X
	North to airport	X				1	1							
	South to Hana			X		4	2							
	Cave Loop	X				100 yards								
6	Hana Town	X				1-2	1-2		73	3	54	2½	X	X X X
7	Helio's Grave			X		.5	½		79	3	60	2½	X X	X X X X
8	Haleakala (Kipahulu Section)								82	3	63	2½		
	Pipiwai		X			1.83	1½	900					X X X X	X X X X X
	Kuloa Loop	X				1	1						X	X X X X
	HALEAKALA ZONE													
9	Haleakala Wilderness (In Volcano)				X				59	2	40	1½	X X X X	X X X
	Sliding Sands					3.9	1½	2300						
	Halemauu					3.9	3	1000						
	Ka Moa O Pele					1.7	1							
	Lauulu					2.3	2½	2000						
	Silversword Loop					.4	½							
	Kaupo Gap					8	3	6400						
	(Volcano Rim)													
	Supply Trail			X		2.5	1½	1000	48	1½	29	1	X X	X
	Hosmer Grove	X				.5	½		48	1½	29	1	X	X X
10	Skyline				X	8	4	3800	59	2	40	1½	X X X X	X X
11	Polipoli Park								50	2	31	1½		
	Redwood	X				1.7	1	900					X X X X X	X X X
	Tie	X				.5	½	500					X X X X X	
	Plum	X				1,7	1½						X X X X X	X X X
	Polipoli	X				.6	½						X X X X	X
	Haleakala Ridge	X				1.6	1	600					X X X X X	X
	Boundary	X				4.0	2½						X X X X X	X X X
	Waiohuli	X				1,4	1½	800					X X X X	X
	Waiakoa			X		7.0	5	1800					X X X X	X
	Waiakoa Loop			X		3	2	500					X X X X	X
	Mamane	X				1.2	1						X X X X	X
	Kahua Road			X		3.5	3						X X X X	X X
12	Waihou Springs + Loop	X				1.5	1½		39	1	17	½	X X X	X
13	Piiholo Hill	X				2	1	560	35	1	16	½	X X X X	X X X X
	SOUTH ZONE													
14	Puu Olai	X				.5	½	360	32	1¼	21	¾	X X	X X X
15	King's Highway (Hoapili)			X		5.5	3		35	1½	24	1	X X X	X X X
	CENTRAL ZONE													
16	Kapaniwai Park	X				100 yards			23	1	2	¼	X	X X X
17	Iao Valley	X							24	1	3	¼		
	Nature Loop	X				100 yards							X	X
	Tableland			X		2	1½	500					X X X X X	X X X X
	Iao Stream	X				1	½						X	X X
18	Cross above Wailuku			X		1	1	1000	23	1	2	¼	X X X	X
19	Kanaha Bird Sanctuary	X				2	1		20	¾	2	¼	X X X	X X
20	Waihee Valley			X		2	1½		31	1¼	10	½	X X X X X	X X X
21	Waihee Ridge			X		3	2	1500	32	1¼	11	½	X X X X	X X X
	WEST ZONE													
22	Kealia Pond	X				2	1		20	½	8	¼	X X	X X
23	Lahaina Pali			X		5.5	3	1600	11	½	6	¼	X X X	X X
24	Olowalu Petroglyphs	X				0.6	½		6	¼	15	½	X X X X	X
25	Lahaina Town	X				1-3	1-3		–	–	21	1	X	X X
26	Lahaina "L"			X		2.5	2	1000	2	¼	21	1	X X X	X X
27	Nakalele Blowhole	X				.5	½		18	¾	39	1½	X	X

PART II:

HIKING TRAILS ON MAUI

Aah! Hiking is so much fun!

TWIN FALLS

Access to Twin Falls is once again open.

This updated edition of Hiking Maui was completed and at the printer when I learned the trail was open. Consequently, it was only possible to include one page of hike/trail information.

Twin Falls is 21 miles from Wailuku off Route 36. Look for a wide shoulder on the right just before Hoolawa Bridge, a large, white bridge past the 2-mile highway marker.

The hike to the falls is an easy one-mile hike for the family. The trail/road is on private land so stay on the road and respect the homesteads found here. DO NOT pick fruit found trailside.

On the trail: Climb over the gate and follow the dirt road into the valley. After a few hundred yards, several paths on the left lead to Hoolawa Stream, a waterfall and a pool. When the stream is full, it's one of the best swimming sites. Residents have tied a rope from a branch of a large banyan tree from which they enjoy swinging over and diving into the pool below.

The trail/road continues into the valley passing numerous homesites on both sides of the road before reaching a hand-painted trail sign at a junction. One trail goes left and up a short rise over a wide, clearly defined path that parallels an irrigation ditch before reaching the largest fall.

The other trail continues on the road for about 50 yards to an irrigation system, crosses over a narrow bridge and follows the bank of a ditch to the second waterfall.

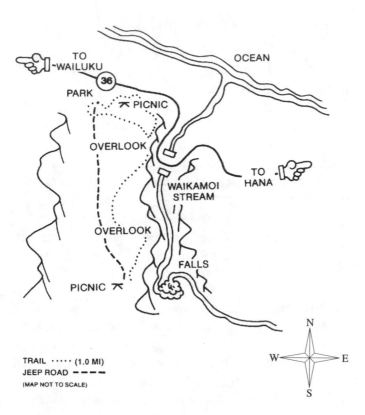

TRAIL ····· (1.0 MI)
JEEP ROAD ————
(MAP NOT TO SCALE)

WAIKAMOI RIDGE
(Hiking Area No. 1)

Zone: East.
Rating: Family.
Features: Native and introduced plants and trees, bamboo forest, picnic tables.
Permission: None.

Hiking Distance & Time: 1 mile, 1/2 hour, 300 foot gain.
Driving Instructions:

From Lahaina (46 miles, 1 1/2 hours) south-east on Route 30, right on Route 38, right on Route 36 to sign "Waikamoi Ridge Trail."   A picnic table is on a 15-foot rise overlooking the parking turnout.

From Wailuku (27 miles, 1 hour) east on Route 32, right on Route 36 to sign "Waikamoi Ridge Trail."

Introductory Notes: The Waikamoi (lit. "water acquired by the threadfish") Ridge Trail is an easy hike for the whole family. Many species of trees and plants can be found here including ash, mahogany, paperbark, hala, tree fern, ti, ginger, philodendron, and strawberry guava to mention a few. There are two picnic areas with tables. One is located at the beginning of the trail, the second on the tableland at the end of the trail. There are two overlooks on the trail which provide views of the highway and Waikamoi Stream.

On the Trail: Walk up the trail to the picnic shelter and walk quietly to the sign, "Quiet, Trees at Work." Pause and enjoy the canopy formed by the branches of giant eucalyptus and paperbark trees from which equally giant philodendron plants seem to reach out for the sky.

Look trailside for edible, tiny, red thimble berries. The trail makes a gentle ascent to a stone/
cement bench from which views of the Hana
Highway below and a large bamboo forest beyond the road are possible. Numerous strawberry guava trees flourish past the lookout. This
golf-ball sized fruit is red with a decidedly strawberry taste. What's more guava contains five
times the vitamin C than oranges.

Of particular interest is a small bamboo forest through which the trail passes before reaching the top of the ridge. Bamboo has long been
an important product on the islands, having been
used for fuel, furniture, fencing, musical instruments, utensils and paper. Indeed, bamboo
sprouts are commonly eaten as a vegetable on
the islands. Walking through the bamboo is especially interesting, for the slightest wind creates a cacophony of sounds.

The trail emerges from the bamboo forest
onto a jeep road that leads to the second picnic
shelter in the shade of several giant mango trees.
Just beyond, a sign marks "Trail' End."

When you decide to return to the trailhead,
you can choose to return on the trail or follow
the jeep road from the second picnic shelter. If
you choose the road, be cautious for it is a steep
descent and, when wet, it can be slippery. Midway down the road you'll pass abandoned ma-
chinery and equipment which was used to construct the East Maui Irrigation system.

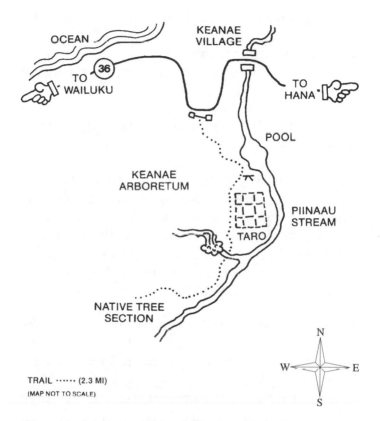

OCEAN

KEANAE VILLAGE

TO WAILUKU

36

TO HANA

POOL

KEANAE ARBORETUM

PIINAAU STREAM

TARO

NATIVE TREE SECTION

TRAIL ······ (2.3 MI)
(MAP NOT TO SCALE)

N
W——E
S

KEANAE ARBORETUM
(Hiking Area No. 2)

Zone: East.
Rating: Family.
Features: Swimming, fruits and native flora (identified).
Permission: None.

Hiking Distance & Time: 2.3 miles, 1 1/2 hours, 200 foot gain.

Driving Instructions:

From Lahaina (53 miles, 2 hours) southeast on Route 30, right on Route 38, right on Route 36 to the arboretum.

From Wailuku (34 miles, 1 1/2 hours) east on Route 32, right on Route 36 to the arboretum.

Introductory Notes: Keanae (lit., "the mullet") Arboretum provides an excellent introduction to native and introduced plants in a setting much like old Hawaii. Three distinct sections feature cultivated Hawaiian plants, native forest trees, and introduced tropical trees. You can enjoy all this and a swim in a fresh water pool.

On the Trail: From the turnstile, a short jeep road (0.2 mile) leads to the gated entrance to the arboretum. Continue on the road or wander among the trees and plants, many of which are labeled. Introduced ornamental timber and fruit trees located in this area are all identified for the visitor. The fruit of the pummelo (Citrus maxima) tree is of particular interest and good taste. It is a large, melon-sized fruit that has the aroma and taste of both grapefruit and orange. There are numerous banana and papaya plants. When you reach a section of planted torch (Etlingera elatior) ginger whose blossom feels like plastic, walk directly to Piinaau (lit., "climb, mount") Stream for the best swimming hole in the arboretum and a delightful picnic spot.

From here, the road is bordered by ti whose soft, pliable leaves are commonly used to make a skirt for hulu dancers. The road leads to an area where several patches of irrigated taro are planted. They represent some of the varieties planted by the Hawaiians. Poi, a native staple, is produced from the taro root.

At the far end of the domestic-plant section and taro patches, a trail (1 mile) leads to a large, forested flat that is representative of a Hawaiian rain forest. The trail is not maintained so that it may be difficult to follow. It winds through some heavy growth in places and crosses a stream a dozen times, offering some welcome relief from the heat. Bear left at the first stream crossing and follow the trail, which parallels the stream below. About 100 yards from the first stream crossing, you will find a few pools suitable for a splash.

Keanae Arboretum Trail

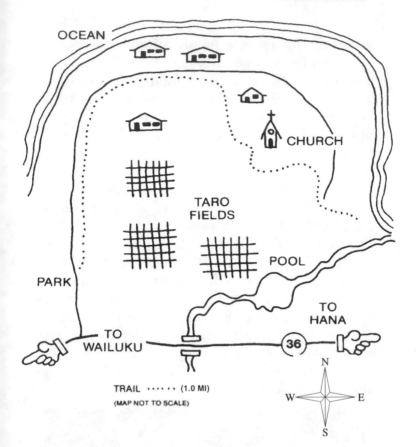

KEANAE VILLAGE
(Hiking Area No. 3)

Zone: East.
Rating: Family.
Features: Hawaiian village, taro, missionary church.
Permission: None.

Hiking Distance & Time: 1 mile, 1/2 hour.
Driving Instructions:
   From Lahaina (53 miles, 2 hours) southeast
on Route 30, right on Route 38, right on Route
36. Just pass the Keanae Arboretum at the bot-
tom of the grade, turn left onto Keanae Village.
   From Wailuku (34 miles, 1 1/2 hours) east on
Route 32, right on Route 36, then as above.

Introductory Notes: The Keanae Village hike
is a short stroll through a Hawaiian village and
fun for the whole family. DO NOT SWIM IN THE
OCEAN. Ocean swells and currents here are extremely dangerous.

On the Trail: Leave your car at one of the two
turnouts on the ocean side of the road. You may
find some local folks throwing a net in the old
Hawaiian way; if so, pause, chat, and investigate their catch. You will find that a smile and a
measure of friendliness will be returned. In spite
of the many signs indicating kapu (keep out),
people in the area will quickly respond to your
interest and conversation. It is a beautiful setting with white, red and yellow plumerias. Hi-
biscus plants and monkeypod trees border the
road, and the ocean crashes against the rugged
lava shores on your left.
   Walk on the road, which makes a half circle
passing home sites and taro fields. With any
luck, you may find someone pounding taro on

the porch or in the yard. Taro is a native staple, cultivated from the earliest times, from which poi, a thick paste, is produced. Hundreds of varieties have been recorded. Poi is made from the tubers (roots), which are baked or boiled and then pounded by hand or machine. It may be eaten fresh or allowed to ferment for a few days, which adds a pleasant sour taste. Poi is traditionally eaten with the fingers along with pork or fish.

The Lanakila Ihiihi O Lehova Ona Kaua (lit., "Sacredness, Success of Jehova, the Son the God") Church on the right side is worth a visit. The church was constructed in 1860, but, like so many missionary churches, it experienced a period of neglect. In 1969 some local people decided to restore it and it was rededicated in July of that year. Now services are held twice a month. On the wall inside the church are newspaper articles and other information that recount the history of the church.

Although the paved road ends at the church, a good gravel road continues along the shoreline to an open space surrounded by hala (Pandanus odoratissimus) which produces a large pineapple-shaped fruit. It is also called "tourist pineapple" since locals jokingly identify it as such to visitors. The crashing surf here is busily crushing the lava shoreline to make black sand. It's a popular tourist stop, but it's also a place to investigate tide pools for their contents. However, be alert, for the surf can sweep up unexpectedly and get you wet or worse.

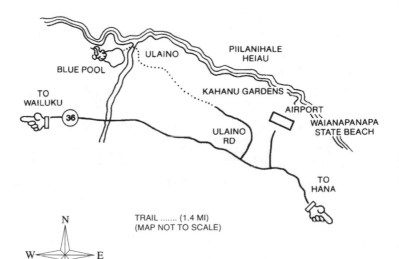

TRAIL .... (1.4 MI)
(MAP NOT TO SCALE)

BLUE POOL
(Hiking Area No. 4)

Zone: East.
Rating: Hardy family.
Features: Swimming pool, waterfall, historical sites.
Permission: None.

Hiking Distance & Time: 1.4 miles, 1 hour.
Driving Instructions:
    From Lahaina (69 miles, 3 hours) southeast
on Route 30, right on Route 38, right on Route
36, left on Ulaino Road just past Rodeo Arena
and 0.5 miles before the Hana Airport Road, and
drive 1.5 miles to a gated entrance to Kahanu
Gardens. Park off-road. When dry, it's possible
to drive the 1.4 miles to the stream just before
Blue Pool.
    From Wailuku (50 miles, 2 hours) east on
Route 32, right on Route 36, then as above.

Introductory Notes: Until recently, Blue Pool
was one of Maui's best kept secrets. The pool
and waterfall were popular with local residents
but unknown to visitors. It's one of the most ex-
quisite spots anywhere. Wow!

On the Trail: Follow the tree-lined, dirt road
from Kahanu Garden. It is a level, cool hike as
the trail passes under a canopy of hala and kukui
or candlenut (Aleurites moluccana) trees. The
latter was introduced to Hawaii by early
Polynesian travelers and is easily identified by
its large maple-like leaves and black, walnut-
sized nut from which popular and attractive
necklaces are made and available in all the shops.
In earlier times, the oil was extracted from the
nut and used for fuel and light. My favorite flowering tree, the tall African tulip (Spathodea

campanulata) with its large, brilliant orange blossoms, is readily identifiable. Be on the lookout for yellow guava and for mangoes.

You will pass several homesteads on both sides of the trail, but the stone walls of the long-since abandoned Ulaino village have been overtaken by the jungle so that they are not recognizable. The village once extended throughout the shoreline area.

The road ends at Heleleikeoha Stream which is usually easy to ford. Find the easiest crossing point and follow the coast for about 150 yards to Blue Pool on the left. Believe me, there is no chance of missing it. You'll "Wow" too! How about a swim and lunch?

Swim time

WAIANAPANAPA STATE PARK
(Hiking Area No. 5)

Zone: East.

Rating: Consult individual hikes.

Features: Lava flows and formations, heiaus, burial sites, swimming, camping, blowholes, caves, black-sand beach.

Permission: For tenting and cabin reservations and permits write Hawaii State Department of Land & Natural Resources, State Parks Division (address in Appendix, and see "Maui's Camp-grounds" and Maui's Housekeeping Cabins" in the Introduction for details).

Hiking Distance & Time: Consult individual hikes.

Driving Instructions:

From Lahaina (70 miles, 3 hours) southeast on Route 30, right on Route 38, right on Route 36, left on road to Waianapanapa State Park.

From Wailuku (51 miles, 2 1/2 hours) east on Route 32, right on Route 36, then as above.

Introductory Notes: A round trip from Wailuku to Hana in one day is exhausting. To enjoy the beauty and serenity of the area, take a couple of days and drive the Hana Highway, camp at Waianapanapa (lit., "glistening water") State Park or secure accommodations in Hana, swim at the black-sand beach, and hike the lava flows to the airport and to Hana.

Cabins situated along the beach are fully fur-

THE WESTIN MAUI
SEA DOGS

7003 MILA

CHK 7941 MAR29'02 3:11PM GST 2

---

1 HOT DOG		5.28
1 TURKEY SAND		6.48
2 SODA @ 2.40		4.80
Food		11.76
Non-Alc		4.80
Tax		0.69
Amt Due		$17.25

Gratuity _____ $1.00

Total _____ $18.25

Room Number _____ 942

Print Name _____ UC

Signature _____

Daily Happy Hour 5-7 PM
at the Ono Surf Bar & Grill

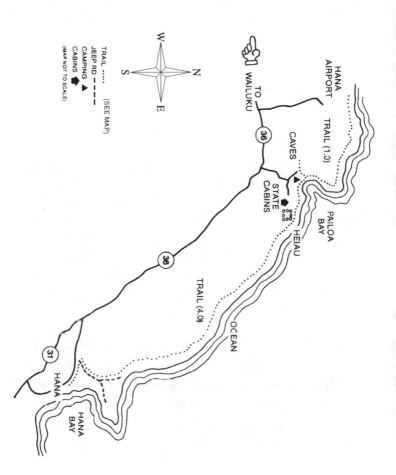

nished and very comfortable. Each has beds, linen, utensils and an electric stove. All you need to bring is food. (See "Maui's Housekeeping Cabins" in the Introduction for details).

North to the Airport, 1 mile, 1 hour
(trail rating: family).

The trail north from the black-sand beach is particularly rough because of the lava rocks underfoot. After passing two small bays, look for Hawaiian burial grounds and a heiau on your left where the terrain levels somewhat. The gravesites on top of the rough aa rock are rather prominent mounds. As you hike, you will be aware of the pounding surf and the interesting formations in the lava rock. Children enjoy assigning names to these strange forms. Be careful, as the trail is often precariously close to the surf. Pause as you walk and look for turtles who are feeding or playfully riding the surf. You are hiking over an early Hawaiian shoreline trail extending to the Piilanihale Heiau some three miles north of the airport.

You may choose to return to Waianapanapa via the shoreline route or to take the paved road by the airport to the Hana Highway and follow it to Waianapanapa.

South to Hana, 4 miles, 2 hours
(trail rating: hardy family).

The trail south begins on a cliff above Pailoa

Waianapanapa Black Sand Beach

(lit., "always splashing") Bay, with its black-sand beach, and follows the coastline - at times coming precariously close to the edge - to the enclosed bay at Hana.

Just below the campground you'll find burial sites decorated with artificial flowers and overlooking a rather fragile lava formation. The lava flow is undoubtedly honeycombed with tunnels and caves, evidenced by the many pits and holes and by the sound of rushing, crashing surf underfoot. Indeed, one blowhole is just a few hundred feet beyond the burial grounds.

The white substance on the lava is called Hawaiian "snow." A lichen, it is the first plant to grow on fresh lava. Other plants along the hike include the hala (Pandanus odoratissimus), which produces a large pineapple-shaped fruit. It is also called "tourist pineapple," since locals jokingly identify it as such to visitors. Beach morning glory (Ipomoea pesca-prae), with its pretty, delicate blue or purple flowers, plays an important role in preventing wind and water erosion of beaches by forming a large carpet. Also, a bush form of sandalwood (Santalum ellipticum) which grows less than three feet high is rather profuse in most areas.

You'll find rental cabins nestled among the hala trees at 0.5 mile, with a number of trails leading from them to the beach. At 0.6 mile a small bridge crosses a natural arch in the lava under which the surf pounds and crashes as small crabs scurry about. Just before the bridge, you may be sprayed by a small blowhole that is particularly active when the surf is up.

Overlooking the sea from its volcanic perch (0.7 mile) is a heiau (a place of worship). Heiaus played an important part in pre-Christian Hawaiian culture. There are hundreds of known heiaus on the islands that served specifically to ensure rain, good crops, or success in war, while others were used for human sacrifice. From the heiau, you pass a generous growth of hala, follow the coastline at its very edge, and reach a point about 50 feet above the surf. From here, about midpoint in the hike, you can see the cross on Mt. Lyons erected in memory of Paul Fagan, founder of the Hana Ranch and Hotel. You can also see tree-covered Kauiki (Lit., "glimmer") Head, an imposing buttress on the south side of Hana Bay.

The trail is no longer clearly identifiable. However, you should not have any problem if you follow the coastline and avoid "ankle twisters" on the broken lava. You will find numerous caves and pits caused by gas that was trapped under the lava as the surface cooled. Later, the brittle surface collapsed, leaving some interesting holes.

When you arrive on a boulder-laden beach, a sign marks the trail's end. From here, you can

Trail to Hana

take any of the roads leading to the Hana Highway for a return trip to Waianapanapa, continue
along the beach for 1/2 mile to Hana Bay, or return to the park via the lava flows. It is worth
the extra hike to Hana Bay for lunch and a swim
at its calm, gray-colored beach. The water at
Hana Bay is not dirty but simply discolored by
decomposed lava.

Waianapanapa Cave Loop, 100 yards,
 (trail rating: family)

Before you leave Waianapanapa, be sure to
take the short hike to the caves, where it is possible to swim underwater to a chamber with a
rock ledge. Legend recounts that a Hawaiian
princess hid in the cave from her jealous hus-
band, who, while resting by the cave, saw her
reflection in the water. Since the ledge in the
cave was a reputed meeting place for lovers, he
promptly slew her by smashing her head against
the walls of the cave. Consequently, it is said,
the water in the pool turns blood-red every April,
and her screams can be heard. If you cannot
accept this legend, you may choose to believe that
the red color of the water is the result of the tiny
red shrimps that frequent the pool, and the
screams are the result of the water and wind
sweeping into the lava tube from the ocean.

HANA TOWN
(Hiking Area No. 6)

Zone: East.

Rating: Family.

Features: "A bit of old Hawaii," museum, historical sites, churches, swimming.

Hiking Distance & Time: 1-2 miles, 1-2 hours (See numbered highlights below and map).

Driving Instructions:

From Lahaina (73 miles, 3 hours) southeast on Route 30, right on Route 38, right on Route 36 to Hana Bay.

From Wailuku (54 miles, 2 1/2 hours) east on Route 32, right on Route 36 to Hana Bay.

Introductory Notes: I recommend that visitors spend one night in Hana so that they may enjoy the Hana Highway with it's many delights, but, more importantly, so that they may enjoy Hana Town, one of the very special places anywhere. You need to spend at least three hours to just enjoy the highlights of this largely Aloha-spirited, Hawaiian community.

Take every opportunity to talk to local people as you stroll through town. They are quick to discuss their home as well as yours. Many locals have traveled extensively or have relatives on the mainland and they always seem to have a relation of friend in your town. In any event, be assured that "Aloha" lives in Hana.

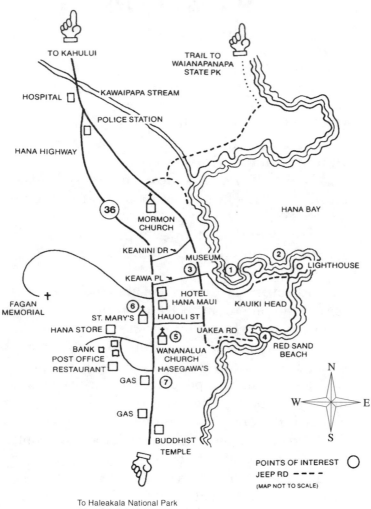

To Haleakala National Park
Oheo Gulch (10 MI)

On the Road:

(1)   HANA BAY. A logical departure point for exploring the town especially if you have driven in the same day. Upon arrival, you may opt to swim in the bay or snooze on the soft gray sand beach. Lunch at Tutu's snack shop offers a lot of local specials like a teriaki-burger or saimen (noodle soup) and, of course, haupia (coconut) ice cream for dessert. Yum ! Yum!

(2)   QUEEN KAAHUMANU'S BIRTH-PLACE. (200 yards from Tutu's). From Tutu's, walk the road toward the pier and at water's edge, follow a dirt path toward the lighthouse (beacon). At this writing, earth slides destroyed most of the path which may prevent you from continuing. Proceed only if you can do so safely. Just before the beacon, a plaque commemorates the birthplace of Queen Kaahumanu, the favorite wife of King Kamehameha. It is believed that the future Queen was born in a cave, perhaps the one above the plaque.

(3)   HALE WAIWAI O'HANA. ("House of Treasures of Hana") (0.2 mile from Tutu's). It may be the tinyest museum in the world but it's fine. Built in 1983, it stands on the grounds of the refurbished, hundred-year-old former county courthouse. Here you'll find many old, rare photographs of Hana, Hawaiian quilts, poi boards, kapa, stone mortars, Hawaiian games, and most importantly, a large measure of "Aloha" from the friendly staff. Look for my favorite exhibit,

"A'i'Ai," a special pohaki (stone) donated by Hawaiian authoress, Inez Ashdown. "He" has per-
fect little ears, nose, mouth, and eyes. Note also
the very beautiful koa wood doors to the museum.

(4)   RED SAND BEACH. (0.5 mile from museum). Walk south on Uakea Road past Hotel
Hana-Maui on the right to the end of the pave-
ment to the parking area for the hotel's beach
units. Turn left across an open field, and descend to the shoreline where you'll find a trail
leading to Kaihalulu (Lit., "roaring sea") Beach,
Hana's popular red sand beach. (CAUTION: THE
UNDERFOOTING IS LOOSE ASH AND HAZ-
ARDOUS) It's also popular with nudists, so be
forewarned if nakedness is offensive. It is a fair
snorkeling spot, but be certain to snorkel and
swim between the beach and rocks which form a
partial buffer from the roaring sea.

(5)   WANANALUA CHURCH.   (0.3 mile
from Red Sand Beach). This interesting, century and a half old church on Hauoli Street was
built by hand of lava rock over a 20-year period.
Information about the restored church is found
inside the entrance.

(6)   ST. MARY'S CATHOLIC CHURCH.
(Across the street from Wananalua Church). A
very beautiful, brightly painted church. As you
face the church, the conspicuous cross on the hill
above the town is a memorial to Paul Fagan, the
founder of the Hana Ranch.

(7)   HASEGAWA GENERAL STORE. (0.2

miles from St. Mary's). If you visit Hana and you don't stop at Hasegawa's store, you have made a BIG mistake. I will not even attempt to describe what you can expect inside. Suffice it to say that Hasegawa's has everything anyone would want to buy. They may not be able to find it under piles of merchandise, but it's there somewhere! Expect a warm "Aloha" from the employees and from owner, Harry Hasegawa. The generosity of the Hasegawa family over the years is legendary.

Harry Hasegawa, Proprietor

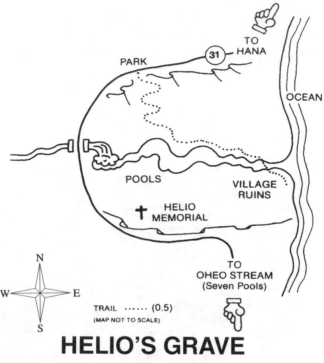

HELIO'S GRAVE
(Hiking Area No. 7)

Zone: East.
Rating: Strenuous. (NOT RECOMMENDED).
Features: Old Hawaiian village, rugged coast-line, swimming pools and natural slide.
Permission: None.
Hiking Distance & Time: 0.5 mile, 1/2 hour.
Driving Instructions:

From Lahaina (79 miles, 3 hours) southeast on Route 30, right on Route 38, right on Route 36 to Hana, right on Route 31 to sign "Helio's Grave."

From Wailuku (60 miles, 2 1/2 hours) east on Route 32, right on Route 36 to Hana, then as above.

Introductory Notes: Helio Kawaloa, one of the first Hawaiian converts to Christianity, converted some 4,000 Mauians in 1840, before the arrival of Catholic priests. A concrete cross on the ridge between the road and the sea is a memorial to him.

On the Trail: THIS TRAIL IS NOT RECOMMENDED BUT IS INCLUDED BECAUSE A ROAD SIGN LOCATES THE TRAIL. THE TRAIL, WHICH IS NOT MAINTAINED AND HEAVILY OVERGROWN, DESCENDS A VERY STEEP BANK. IF YOU CHOOSE TO HIKE, PROCEED WITH CAUTION. The trail begins behind an interpretive Hawaiian Visitors Bureau marker and is in fact a "slide" on all fours and not a hike to the valley floor. From there, the stream and the shoreline are easy to find. Across the stream is the abandoned village of Wailua (lit., "two waters"), whose walls are in good condition and provide the visitor with an idea of the physical layout of an old Hawaiian village.

Follow the stream for a few hundred feet inland from the village to swim in the pools and to slide down a natural slide, which is a lot of fun even though it is not as smooth as one would wish. One disadvantage is the presence of mosquitoes - use plenty of repellent.

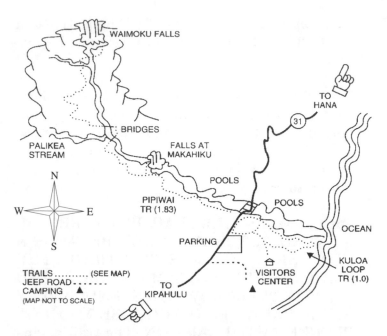

HALEAKALA NATIONAL PARK
(Kipahulu Section)
(Hiking Area No. 8)

Zone: East.

Rating: See individual hikes.

Features: Waimoku Falls, Falls at Makahiku, bamboo forest, ancient Hawaiian agricultural sites, swimming, fruit, Oheo Stream, free camping.

Permission: None to hike or camp.

Hiking Distance & Time: See individual hikes.

Driving Instructions:

  From Lahaina (82 miles, 3 hours) southeast

Pools at Oheo - Haleakala National Park

on Route 30, right on Route 38, right on Route
36 to Hana. Continue on Route 31 to Haleakala
National Park, Kipahulu Section.

From Wailuku (63 miles,2 1/2 hours) east on
32, right on Route 36, then as above.

Introductory Notes: The Hana Highway and
the pools in Oheo Gulch (popularly known as the
Seven Sacred Pools) are two of the most popular
tourist attractions on the island. To avoid a tir-
ing return trip to Central Maui the same day,
you should consider staying at the cabins or
campgrounds outside Hana at Waianapanapa
State Park or camping in the National Park (see
"Maui's Campgrounds" and "Maui's Housekeeping Cabins" in the Introduction for details). The
Park Service campground is located on pasture
land south of the pools on a bluff overlooking the
rugged coastline. There is no water or amenities
available. Chemical toilets are placed throughout the parking area. Camping is free and no
permits are required.

The National Park Service rangers conduct a
hike to Waimoku Falls every Saturday, departing from the Ranger Station at 9 :30 a.m. sharp.

Pipiwai Trail, 1.83 miles, 1 1/2 hours,
900 foot gain (trail rating: hardy family).

On the Trail: Begin your hike at the Ranger
Station and walk north to the trailhead (posted).

The trail goes left and passes through a wooded area to the highway. On the opposite side of the road, the trail ascends under a guava tree forest paralleling the stream below. Sample the yellow, lemon-sized guava while hiking. The fruit contains five times the amount of Vitamin C than an orange. A few hundred yards from the trailhead stands a 10-foot-tall concrete support, which is all that remains of a water-flume system that once spanned Oheo Gulch and carried sugar cane to a now abandoned sugar mill one mile away in Kipahulu. The first highlight along the trail, however, is at the 0.5 mile point, where the 184-foot Falls at Makahiku drops into a stunning gorge below. To the left of the lookout, an abandoned irrigation ditch cut in the cliff allows you to hike to the top of the falls.

At the one-mile point, the trail reaches two newly constructed bridges, one over Pipiwai Stream and the other over Oheo Stream. Here you are likely to find daring young men and women leaping from the pali into the water below. USE EXTREME CAUTION if you choose to follow their practice.

Beyond the bridges, the trail is always wet and muddy. It is well-defined, but expect to hop over slippery rocks, and to carefully avoid the exposed roots on the trail. The Park Service has placed sections of boardwalk in the muddiest places.

The trail takes you through three marvelous bamboo forests. If the wind is up, you'll be ser-

enaded by a discordant symphony of rattling
bamboo. Beyond this "musical" forest are the
remains of old taro patches, evidenced by walled
terraces and shelter sites. Additionally, there
are edible thimbleberries, coffee plants and, of
course, guavas. With luck you will also find ripe
mountain apples (Eugenia malaccensis). Before
the falls there are numerous trees that bear a
small, deep-crimson fruit with a pure white pulp
and a large, round seed.

Shortly, Waimoku Falls comes into view. It's
an idyllic spot to picnic after a pleasant hike.
USE CAUTION if you opt to shower under the
falls,. Remember, most of the rocks in the stream
fell from above.

Kuloa Loop, 1 mile,1 hour
(trail rating: family).

On the Trail: Everyone loves the pools, and every visitor on the island seems to be there! From
the parking lot, follow the trail toward the visitors center that contains several displays and a
ranger who can answer questions regarding the
Park. Walk north from the center to a junction
where the Pipiwai Trail goes left and Kuloa Loop
Trail goes right. Picnic tables are stationed in
shady places trailside until you reach the pools.
Continue on the trail toward the ocean until you
reach a bluff overlooking the Pools of Oheo. The
pools are usually crowded between the hours of
11 a.m. and 3 p.m. A crudely made staircase leads
to the pools below. Here you're likely see young

men and women diving and leaping from the bank and even from the bridge high above the water. CAUTION: Enjoy the pools, but be cautious when swimming or diving. Several deaths and serious accidents have occurred here in recent years. The nearest medical facilities are ten miles distant in Hana.

The loop trail ascends the south side of the stream and leads to the highway and the bridge from which marvelous views are possible upstream and downstream to the ocean. The pools upstream are usually less crowded than downstream. CAUTION: DO NOT enter the pools during high or fast moving water. Be alert; Water in the stream can rise quickly.

From the road retrace you steps to the trail junction where one trail continues along the stream and the trail to the parking lot goes right completing the loop.

On the trail

HALEAKALA NATIONAL PARK
(Wilderness)
(Hiking Area No. 9)

Zone: Haleakala.

Rating: Strenuous hiking into wilderness.

Features: "Moon" hiking, silversword, nene goose (State bird of Hawaii), lava tubes, lava formations, rental cabins, camping.

Permission: Entrance fee to Park. Hiking and cabin permits from Haleakala National Park. (See "Maui's Campgrounds" and "Maui's Housekeeping Cabins" in the Introduction for details).

Hiking Distance & Time: See the mileage tables in the text below.

Driving Instructions:

From Lahaina (59 miles, 2 hours) southeast on Route 30, right on Route 38, right on Route 36, right on Route 37, left on Route 377, left on Route 378 to the summit.

From Wailuku (40 miles, 1 1/2 hours) east on Route 32, right on Route 36, right on Route 37, left on Route 377, then as above.

Introductory Notes: As you drive to the summit of Haleakala look for the large (three-foot) ring-necked pheasant (Phasianus colchicus torquatus) and the smaller chukar (Alectoris graeca) with its brownish black markings and a black band extending through each eye and joining at the lower throat. Both flush along the road and may also be seen in the park.

"Give me my life," pleads the sun after Maui, the demigod, has lassoed it. "I will give you your life," replies Maui, "if you promise to go more slowly across the sky so the women may dry their cloth." To this day, the sun seems to pass more slowly over Haleakala, the House of the Sun. Such legends are still repeated by locals when they speak of nature's cauldron of power and destruction that helped create their island.

Recent evidence, however, credits other forces. Scientists believe that a hot spot exists beneath the earth's crust in the Pacific area and, as a consequence of periodic eruptions of this hot spot, a chain of volcanoes, the Hawaiian Islands,

On the Moon?

has been created. Centuries of submarine volcanic eruptions piled up successive layers of lava.
Finally, this undersea volcano burst through the
ocean's churning surface, and eventually reached
a height of 15,000 feet above the Pacific Ocean.
Nature then began to work her wonders from
above, as wind, rain and the sea eroded the new
rock, and streams ripped away at its surface, creating valleys. Ultimately, in the Haleakala area,
two major valleys grew until they met, forming
a long depression. Subsequent volcanic activity
then filled the depression, while vent eruptions
created symmetrical cones. Today, Haleakala
stands proudly at 10,023 feet. Nevertheless,
Haleakala is not extinct but only dormant, and
it can be expected to erupt again some day.

The persistent trade winds, carrying over 300
inches of rain per year, had an equally dramatic
effect on Haleakala Volcano. Because these
winds blow consistently in one direction, the volcano has eroded unequally, and the vegetation
differs correspondingly. Erosion has created two
gaps in the volcano: the Kaupo Gap on the south
side, and the steeper Koolau Gap on the north
side. It is possible to hike down the Kaupo Gap.

Statistically, the "House of the Sun" is a large
dormant volcano, covering an area of 19 square
miles. It is 7 1/2 miles long, 2 1/2 miles wide,
and 21 miles in circumference. Experts do not
regard the "crater" as a true volcanic crater since
thousands of years of erosion have carved a val-

ley. Park officials no longer refer to the "depression" as a "crater" but as a "valley" which they now refer to as the "wilderness." Some 36 miles of well-marked trails invite the hiker to enjoy the awesome yet delicate beauty, and the unmatched serenity and solitude of the valley/wilderness area.

Hiking into the wilderness is serious business because of the distance involved, the terrain, the altitude and the temperature which commonly ranges between 40-65 degrees Fahrenheit. Below freezing temperatures with a wind-chill factor are not uncommom at any time . Another consideration is hypothermia, which sets in when the body is not able to generate enough heat to keep the vital organs warm. Hypothermia can be fatal, so that visitors are well-advised to carry warm clothing — shoes, jacket, long pants — even during the summer. Water is available at the cabins in the wilderness, but IT MUST BE TREATED OR BOILED.

If your schedule allows, choose a day with a full moon and hike into the wilderness in the evening. During the summer months, the temperature ranges from 35 to 77 degrees Fahrenheit so that warm clothing is essential, but the experience is marvelous.

Park rules require that wilderness hikers adhere to the following:

1. Hiking off-trail and shortcutting switchbacks is prohibited.

2. Collecting anything is prohibited.
3. To protect the environment and assure solitude, group size is limited to 12 persons for all hiking and camping.
4. No pets allowed in the wilderness or on trails.
5. Firearms, motors, radios, bicycles, wheeled vehicles, and open fires are prohibited in the wilderness.
6. Pack out everything you pack in.
7. Do not feed or harass the nene or any wildlife.
8. Use pit toilets at campgrounds or cabins.

Experienced hikers can plan a trip from the information contained herein. For others, I recommend the following hikes.

PART-DAY HIKE

Sliding Sands Trail to Kaluu o Ka oo

An enjoyable 3-4 hour, 5-mile round-trip hike can be made by good hikers partway into the wilderness via the Sliding Sands Trail. From the trailhead, you descend 2 miles and 1,400 feet into the wilderness to a posted junction. A 0.5-mile spur trail leads to Kaluu o Ka oo (lit., "the plunge of the digging stick"), which is the only place in Haleakala that you can stand atop a cinder cone and look into the depression on the top. Remember that the return ascent to the summit is demanding at this altitude.

Sliding Sands Trailhead

FULL-DAY HIKES

Halemauu Trail to Holua Cabin.

This is a vigorous, eight-mile-round-trip, 1,400 foot-gain hike over a foot and horse trail to the floor of the valley. Food and water are a must on the trail, although water (treat it) is available at Holua Cabin.

Sliding Sands Trail to Holua Cabin, exit by Halemauu Trail.

If you only have one day and if you want to hike into the wilderness and if you are a good hiker in good physical condition, then this it the hike for you. It's a difficult 11-mile, 1,400-foot-gain one-day hike, but it will take you down the marvelous Sliding Sands trail, across the valley floor, and up the Halemauu Trail. Whew! Better yet, plan an overnight stay at Holua Cabin or campground.

OVERNIGHT HIKES

Sliding Sands Trail to Holua Cabin, exit by Halemauu Trail. (see previous description)

This is a pleasant hike, and moderately strenuous when it includes an overnight stay in a rustic cabin. Tenting in the campground near the cabin is permitted. Remember, advance reservations are necessary to secure Holua cabin.

Sliding Sands Trail to Kapalaoa Cabin, exit by Halemauu Trail.

This hearty, 13.5-mile hike features an overnight visit at Kapalaoa Cabin. In the morning you can traverse the valley floor, visiting Pele's Paint Pot and the Silversword Loop, and then exit via Halemauu Trail.

Sliding Sands Trail to Paliku Cabin to Kaupo Village.

Hikers in good condition can take this 17.5-mile hike from the highest point on Maui to sea level. It covers the sparsely vegetated crater and the lush foliage of the Kaupo Gap. An overnight visit at Paliku is particularly rewarding, since the rich flora there is in marked contrast to the rest of the Park.

If you are able to spend more than one night in the wilderness, I recommend staying at Holua or Paliku Cabins. Time permitting, spend a night at each cabin. This will certainly enable you to enjoy the Park at a leisurely pace.

TRAIL MILEAGE

Sliding Sands Trail
Summit at 9,745 feet to:

Holua Cabin	7.4
Kapalaoa Cabin	5.8
Paliku Cabin	9.8
Kaupo Village	17.5

Halemauu Trail
Park road at 8,000 feet to:

Holua Cabin	3.9
Silversword Loop	4.8
Kawilinau	6.2
Kapalaoa Cabin	7.7
Paliku Cabin	10.2
Kaupo Village	17.9

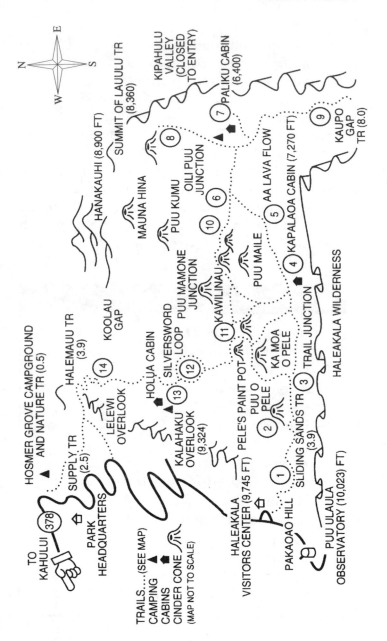

TO KAHULUI 378

PARK HEADQUARTERS

TRAILS.....(SEE MAP)
CAMPING
CABINS
CINDER CONE
(MAP NOT TO SCALE)

HOSMER GROVE CAMPGROUND AND NATURE TR (0.5)

SUPPLY TR (2.5)

HALEMAUU TR (3.9)

KOOLAU GAP

LELEWI OVERLOOK

HOLUA CABIN

KALAHAKU OVERLOOK (9,324)

SILVERSWORD LOOP

PELE'S PAINT POT

PUU O PELE

KA MOA O PELE

HALEAKALA VISITORS CENTER (9,745 FT)

SLIDING SANDS TR (3.9)

PAKAOAO HILL

PUU ULAULA OBSERVATORY (10,023) FT)

TRAIL JUNCTION

HALEAKALA WILDERNESS

PUU MAILE

KAPALAOA CABIN (7,270 FT)

AA LAVA FLOW

KAWILINAU

PUU MAMONE JUNCTION

PUU KUMU

OILI PUU JUNCTION

MAUNA HINA

HANAKAUHI (8,900 FT)

SUMMIT OF LAUULU TR (8,360)

KIPAHULU VALLEY (CLOSED TO ENTRY)

PALIKU CABIN (6,400)

KAUPO GAP TR (8.0)

① ② ③ ④ ⑤ ⑥ ⑦ ⑧ ⑨ ⑩ ⑪ ⑫ ⑬ ⑭

On the Trail: The following description of trails and highlights encountered along the way correspond to the numbers on the map. Six interconnected trails in the wilderness are listed on the hiking chart.

1. Sliding Sands Trail

The trail begins just above the visitor center on the south side of Pakaoao at 9,740 feet and descends 2500 feet in four miles to the valley floor. Pause before descending for a broad panorama of the Park. With the map, a number of prominent points can be identified. Koolau (lit., "windward") Gap is to the north and Kaupo Gap is south of Paliku.

Pakaoao has an interesting history as a place used by wayfarers and by robbers who waylaid them. The southwest slope was once covered with stone-walled enclosures used by the Hawaiians as sleeping shelters and for protection from the elements.

As you begin your hike, you will agree that the Sliding Sands Trail is appropriately named. The cinders and ash that make up the area around the trail were expelled from vents during eruptions and were carried by the wind to line the inner volcano. As you descend, the contrasts of the volcano become evident. The lush forest of the Koolau Gap to the north and the usually cloud-enshrouded Kaupo Gap southeast stand in marked contrast to the seemingly barren terrain around you.

After 2 miles and a 1,700-foot descent, you reach a trail marker which identifies a spur trail that leads to Kaluu o Ka oo, a cinder cone. At the end of this short spur trail, you stand atop a cinder cone and examine its design close up.

You will find some common plants in this area. The pukiawe (Styphelia tameiameiae) has tiny, evergreen-like leaves with reddish-white berries. The plant with yellowish flowers on up-right stems is the kupaoa (Dubautia menziesii) which, literally translated, means "fragrant." A few isolated silversword plants (see Haleakala Trail Description No. 12) are located just off the trail.

2. Puu O Pele ("Hill of Pele")

Although legend has it that Pele, the Hawai-ian goddess of fire, lives in Kilauea Volcano on the island of Hawaii, this hill was named in her honor. With binoculars, you are able to see Paliku Cabin in the distance. The building vis-ible to the north is not Holua Cabin but a horse corral used by maintenance crews.

3. Trail Junction

You have hiked 3.9 miles and are now on the valley floor at 7,400 feet. Until recently, you could hear and see goats in the wilderness. The Park Service has since completed a fencing program to keep goats out of the park, but they are found outside. The goats are descendants of those brought to the islands by Captain George Vancouver in the late 1700s. While they seem to delight and entertain visitors, they create a number of problems, since they would eat the silversword, mamane and other desirable vegetation.

Flora in the area includes a native grass (Trisetum glomeratum) that grows in tufts or bunches and is known locally as mountain pili (lit., "cling, stick"). Mountain pilo (lit., "bad odor") (Coprosma montana) is common and may be identified by its orange berries and handsome bush. A favorite of foraging pigs is the bracken fern (Pteridium aquilinum), a fern found in many lands that may be familiar to you.

TRAIL MILEAGE (from the Junction)	
East to:	
Kapalaoa Cabin	1.9
Paliku Cabin	6.0
Kaupo Village	13.7
North via Ka Moa O Pele Trail to:	
Kawilinau	1.7
Holua Cabin	3.5

4. Kapalaoa Cabin (7,270 feet)

Kapalaoa (lit., "the whale or whale tooth") Cabin is one of three comfortable cabins maintained by the Park Service. There is no tent camping permitted in this area.

5. Aa Lava Flow

The hike to Paliku Cabin (3.5 miles) crosses a lava flow composed of aa (lit., "stony") lava, a Hawaiian term that is accepted today by geologists to identify lava whose surface cooled, hardened and fractured into rough pieces. The trail is difficult, with extremely rough underfooting.

Hawaiian "snow," the whitish lichen mentioned in Hiking Area No. 5, is very common on the aa lava. About midpoint, Paliku Cabin is visible straight ahead across the lava flow, nestled in a grove of native trees.

6. Oili Puu ("hill to appear") Junction

Get out the poncho, if you have not already, for the rainy portion of your wilderness experience usually begins at this point if you are going on to Paliku Cabin. A different type of lava (pahoehoe) appears in this area. It is a smooth variety that frequently forms lava tubes when the outside chills and hardens and then the still-molten interior flows out of the cool shell.

Very pretty mamane (Sophora chrysophylli) trees are conspicuous with their yellow blossoms. Hikers favor the fruit of the ohelo (Vaccinium reticulatum) bush, which bears a tasty red, edible berry in the late summer. It is rather prolific in this section of the Park.

Although the jet-black berries of the kukaenene (lit., "goose dung") (Coprosma ernodeoides) bush are eaten by the nene, the Ha-

TRAIL MILEAGE (from the Junction)	
East to:	
Paliku Cabin	1.3
Kaupo Village	9.1
Northwest to:	
Kawilinau	2.7
Holua Cabin	5.0
Park Road	
via Halemauu Trail	8.9

waiian goose, they are used as an emetic by Hawaiians. You are well-advised to avoid them.

7. Paliku Cabin (6,400 feet)

Unless you have cabin reservations or a water-repellent tent and sleeping bag, you won't spend too much time enjoying Paliku (lit., "vertical cliff"). The rain and wind blow for a while, stop, and then start again. It is precisely this yearly 300-plus inches of rain, however, that creates a lush garden of native and introduced plants and makes Paliku the most enchanting spot in the Park. The cabin is located at the base of a pali (lit., "cliff") that towers 1,000 feet above. The campground is in a grassy area to the front-right of the cabin.

Behind the cabin and surrounding the pit toilet, the akala (lit., "pink") (Rubus hawaiiensis), a Hawaiian raspberry, grows profusely. It bears a large, dark, edible berry that is rather bitter to eat but makes a delicious jam. In addition to the mamane described above, other native trees include the ohia (Metrosideros polymorpha), the island's most common native tree, with its gray-green leaves and red flowers that look like those of the bottle-brush plant. The kolea (lit., "boast") (Myrsine lessertiana) is conspicuous around Paliku, since it grows to a height of 50 feet and has thick leaves and dark purplish-red or black fruit. Hawaiians used the sap of the bark to produce a red dye for tapa cloth. Several Methley plum trees are mixed in with the foliage. When ripe, usually May-June, these deep purple, ping-pong-sized fruits are a special treat. In recent years, however, the area has become overgrown and some of the branches of the plum trees have been broken so that fruit has been scarce.

Throughout the Park, look for the nene (Branta sandvicensis), the state bird of Hawaii. After disappearing, this native bird was reintroduced on Maui in 1962 and has since done fairly well. The Park Service has a program to raise goslings and to return them to the wilds in due course. The natural breeding cycle is difficult, owing in part to a number of introduced predators such as mongooses, pigs, and feral dogs and cats, for whom the eggs and the young goslings are easy prey.

Nene - State Bird of Hawaii

The nene has adapted to its rugged habitat on the rough lava flows far from any standing or running water. The most noticeable anatomical change has been a reduction of webbing between the toes, creating a foot that better suits its terrestrial life.

If you are fortunate enough to spot a nene, don't be surprised if it walks up to you. They are very friendly birds. But please, DO NOT FEED them. They are wild animals and they have sufficient food available in the Park.

8. Lauulu Trail

The trail begins behind Paliku Cabin and zig-zags 2.3 miles up the north wall. Although the trail is not maintained, a "good" hiker can make it. Kipahulu (lit., "fetch from exhausted gardens") Valley lies beyond the pali and extends to the ocean. It is a genuine wilderness area that has been explored by a few daring souls who have hiked the difficult Lauulu (lit., "lush") Trail to Kalapawili (lit., "twisting") Ridge. From the ridge there are excellent views of the Hana coast, the Kaupo Gap and the Park. **THIS IS A DEAD-END TRAIL. HIKING INTO KIPAHULU VALLEY IS PROHIBITED.**

9. Kaupo Gap

Kaupo (lit., "night landing") Trail follows Kaupo Gap and is a popular exit from the wilderness portion of the Park, but one that presents a transportation problem from Kaupo Village to central Maui or to Lahaina and Hana. Although the road has been improved around the south side of Kaupo Village, it remains rugged and bumpy. Hitchhiking from Kaupo is only a remote possibility, since few cars are found on the road. However, if you are up to a nine-mile hike to Kipahulu, a ride from there to your destination is more likely.

The trail is well-defined and initially follows the base of the pali, from which a number of waterfalls and cascades during rainy periods are visible, as well as views of the coastline and the Kaupo area. You are using some muscles you didn't use in the volcano, for your descent is 6,000 feet in eight miles, which means you will be "braking" all the way. You may hear goats and pigs along the trail, although they may not be visible in the heavy brush.

About halfway, the trail becomes a jeep road, used by the Kaupo Ranch, which may be used by four-wheel-drive vehicles with permission. The road continues to the trailhead where another road descends to the main road, a short distance from the Kaupo Store.

10. Aa Lava Flow

On the connecting trail between the east and west sides, you are crossing the ancient divide between the Koolau and Kaupo valleys, in addition to one of the most recent lava flows in the crater, which is 500-1000 years old. Just before the trail junction, on the north side, is a prominent wall constructed of lava rock which was once used to corral cattle being driven into the valley to graze on the lush, rich grasses at Paliku.

At the junction, the vertical, slablike columns of rock protruding from the ridge are volcanic dikes that are remnants of the ancient divide between the valleys. Puu Nole (lit., "weak hill") opposite the dikes is a small cinder cone with a number of silversword plants on its slopes.

11. Kawilinau

In recent years a safety railing has been built around this pit, which is 10 feet in diameter and only 65 feet deep. Some locals claim the pit extends to the sea. The pit was formed by superheated gases that blasted through from beneath.

In an earlier period, Hawaiians threw the umbilical cords of their newborn children into this pit to prevent (they believed) the children from becoming thieves or to ensure them strong bodies later in life. The Hawaiians' motive for this practice varied.

As you continue on the trail northwest about 100 yards beyond the pit, look for Pele's Paint Pot, a colorful area that was created by the many different minerals present in the magma. Some people, however, believe that after painting the volcano, Madame Pele discarded her excess paint here. Many volcanic "bombs," hunks of lava in spherical shapes, are identifiable.

12. Silversword Loop

Don't fail to hike this short (0.4 mile) loop trail to view some of the best examples of silversword in the crater. Silversword (Argyroxiphium sandwicense) is probably the single most popular attraction in the crater. The plant is endemic to the islands and, thanks to protection by the Park Service, it is recovering and thriving. Its enemies are "feral" visitors, who pick the firm, silver-colored leaves for souvenirs.

Silversword - Wow!

A relative of the sunflower, the silversword has stiff, stiletto-shaped leaves and a brilliant flower stalk. Typically, the plant will grow from four to twenty years, its age marked by the size and number of silverswords at the base. Then in a brilliant burst, the flower stalk will grow from one to nine feet in height, sometime between May and October, and will produce hundreds of purplish sunflower like blooms. After flowering only once, the entire plant dies and the seeds are left to reproduce. The species does surprisingly well, surviving on 16-50 inches of rain annually. Viewers familiar with the yucca blossom of the Southern California desert will find the silversword familiar, although the two plants are not related. Please stay on the trail when viewing the silversword. The roots are close to the surface and can be easily damaged causing the plant to die.

Holua Cabin

13. Holua Cabin

A day or two's stay is particularly enjoyable at Holua (lit., "sled"). Behind the cabin, about 25 feet up the cliff, is a cave that Hawaiians once used as a campsite. About 100 yards to the front-right of the cabin is a lava tube through which you may walk with the aid of a flashlight. It is about 150 feet long and exits through a hole in the roof. A recent archeological survey found the remains of an adult male and two young children entombed in the portion of the tube between the entrance and spatter vent-known as Na Piko Haua (lit., "the hiding place of the navel cords"). Ancient Hawaiians hid the umbilical cords of their newborn in such pits. It was regarded as unlucky for the child if the cords were found.

TRAIL MILEAGE (from Holua)

East to:

Silversword Loop	0.9
Pele's Paint Pot	2.2
Kawilinau	2.3
Kapalaoa Cabin	3.8
Paliku Cabin	6.3
Kaupo Village	14.1

North to:

Park Road via Halemauu Trail	3.9

At dusk, be certain to listen for the strange call of the dark-rumped petrel (Pterodroma phaeopygia), which sounds like the barking of a small dog. This white-and-black sea bird makes its nest on the volcano's inner slopes, where it produces one white egg annually. For six months afterward, it flies in from the ocean each day to tend the nest, arriving after sundown. It's "bark" seems to assist it in finding the nest after night-fall. This rare creature is now threatened by rats which have invaded the park.

14. Halemauu Trail

Halemauu (lit., "grass hut") Trail, constructed by the Civilian Conservation Corps in the 1930s, remains in good condition. Horse and mule pack trains enter and exit the wilderness via Halemauu on a series of switch-backs for most of the 3.9-mile course, ascending 1,400 feet to the park road at 8,000 feet and 3.5 miles from Park Headquarters.

After a night's rest at Holua Cabin, the hike out offers spectacular views of the Park and the east side when the weather is clear. There are a number of comfortable spots at which to rest in the morning shade. Keep a sharp eye out for the Maui wormwood shrub (Artemisia mauiensis), which is two to three feet high and usually grows on the cliff. It has aromatic silvery leaves and small orange flowers. Hawaiians still pound the leaves to use in treating asthma.

Once on the rim of the volcano, the trail levels somewhat and begins a gradual ascent passing through a gate in a fence constructed to keep goats out of the wilderness. The trail then passes the Supply Trail on the right and continues on to the trailhead.

Hosmer Grove Nature Loop, 0.5 mile, 1/2 hour (trail rating: family)

The grove contains a small campground and picnic area with six tables, fire grills and a tenting area. It is a delight for an overnight visit. It's a good, convenient spot to camp if you wish to see the sunset or the sunrise from the summit of Haleakala. The campground is wheelchair accessible. Camping is free and permits are not required.

A short, 0.5 mile, self-guiding trail is adjacent to the campground, and trail pamphlets are available to assist in identifying the native and introduced plants. Many of the introduced plants were established by Dr. Ralph S. Hosmer, the first Territorial Forester of Hawaii. There are excellent examples of sugi (Japanese cedar), cypress cedar, juniper, Douglas fir, eucalyptus spruce and a number of pines. Native plants include sandalwood, mamane, aalii, mountain pilo, oheo and kupaoa.

Supply Trail, 2.5 miles, 1 1/2 hours, 1000-foot gain (trail rating: strenuous)

The Supply Trail connects hikers and campers in Hosmer Grove with the Halemauu Trail,
which takes you into the wilderness of Haleakala
National Park. The trailhead (posted) is located
on the southside of the road a short distance before reaching the main park road from Hosmer
Grove. From here the mostly rough
(underfooting) trail ascends 1000 feet to the
Halemauu Trail.

Initially, the trail is wide and easy to follow,
but the underfooting is a mixture of lava rock
and volcanic ash. A hat and sunscreen offer some
protection from the sun's rays. Bright yellow
evening primrose (Oenethera stricta) flowers
flourish trailside and throughout most of the
Park. Look also for ohia lehua (Metrosideros
polymorpha), the island's most common native
tree. The bright red blossom is a favorite of Madame Pele, goddess of fire and volcanoes. Legend holds that if the blossom is picked on the
way to the mountain, it will rain. However, it
may be picked on a return trip without risk.

About midway, your trail reaches an abandoned road. The trail continues on the opposite
side and soon passes a rain shed and water tanks.
Weather permitting, views of the eastside are
possible. At the trail junction, the trail to the
right goes to the Halemauu Trailhead and the
main road. Follow the trail to the left to several
magnificent viewpoints into the volcano.

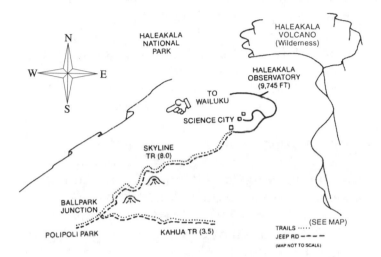

SKYLINE TRAIL

(Hiking Area No. 10)

Zone: Haleakala.

Rating: Strenuous.

Features: Views of Lanai, Kahoolawe and Hawaii, and West Maui Mountains, cinder cones, historical sites, Polipoli Park, and native and imported flora.

Permission: None.

Hiking Distance & Time: 8 miles, 4 hours (to Polipoli Park), 3,800-foot descent.

Driving Instructions:
   From Lahaina (59 miles, 2 hours) southeast
on Route 30, right on Route 38, right on Route
36, right on Route 37, left on Route 377, left on
Route 378 to the summit (Park headquarters is
11 miles before the summit.
   From Wailuku (40 miles, 1 1/2 hours) east on
Route 32, right on Route 36, then as above.

Introductory Notes: Skyline Trail begins on
the south side of Science City. As you approach
the summit and Puu Ulaula (lit., "red hill") Observatory, a road on the left leads to Science City,
where, a hundred yards farther, another road
bears left, marked by a sign indicating the park
boundary. Follow this road to a sign which identifies the Skyline Trail. At this point, you are at
the 9,750-foot level on the southwest rift of
Haleakala Volcano. As noted on the sign, the
jeep road is ordinarily closed to vehicles because
the instruments used in astronomical research
at Science City are sensitive to dust.
   On a clear day, the big island of Hawaii can
be viewed to the southeast. The island of
Kahoolawe (lit., "carrying away by current"),
seven miles off the coast, is uninhabited and until
1991 was used by the military for bombing practice. Known locally as the "Cursed Island,"
Kahoolawe was once used as a base by opium
smugglers. The ghost of a poisoned smuggler is
said to walk at night. Between Maui and
Kahoolawe, tiny, U-shaped Molokini (lit., "many

Skyline Trail to summit

ties") appears. Lanai is to the northwest.

On the Trail: On this trail you will descend a total of 3,800 feet. Be alert for mountain bikers who share the trail. The first 1,000 feet is your "moon walk" over rugged and barren terrain, with several cinder cones and craters along the rift. You are compensated, however, by a spectacular panorama of the island. The eye easily sweeps the offshore islands, the West Maui Mountain range, central Maui and the east side. The Maui "neck" is clearly visible from the trail.

The mamane (lit., "sex appeal") tree line begins at the 8,600-foot level, and the native scrub becomes denser and more varied. A mamane tree (Sophora chrysophylla) in full bloom is a beautiful sight, with its bright yellow flowers. It is a favorite of feral goats, who eat them greedily and quickly exterminate them in an area. The gate across the jeep trail at the 8,200-foot level marks the halfway point to Polipoli. When you reach this point, you will have hiked four miles.

An additional two miles brings you to the Papaanui-Kahikinui (lit., "large, parched-great Tahiti") Junction at 7,000 feet. On the left of the trail is a large open area that was used as a base-ball field by members of the Civilian Conserva-tion Corps during the 1930s. The area is referred to as "Ballpark Junction" by locals. From the junction, it is a one-mile trek to a point where a sign identifies the Haleakala Ridge Trail. After 0.3 mile from the sign, take the Polipoli Trail to the camping area some 0.6 mile farther, passing through dense stands of cypress, cedar and pine.

Polipoli Park provides camping facilities, wa-ter, flush toilets-and a stand of redwood trees. There are also numerous easy family hiking trails in the vicinity (see Hiking Area No.11). Between May and July, delicious Methley plums are a favorite of locals, who swarm over the area in search of the fruit. Unhappily, many trees have been damaged by pickers or overwhelmed by vegetation so the pickings are poor. All along the trail, you can expect to be surprised by Cali-fornia quails, with their curved head plume, ring-necked pheasants, and chukars, which are brownish-black ground-dwelling partridges.

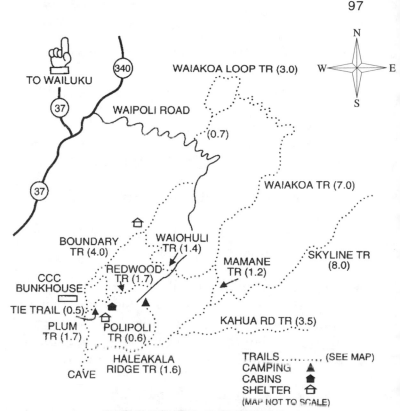

TO WAILUKU

WAIPOLI ROAD

WAIAKOA LOOP TR (3.0)

(0.7)

WAIAKOA TR (7.0)

BOUNDARY
TR (4.0)

WAIOHULI
TR (1.4)

MAMANE
TR (1.2)

SKYLINE TR
(8.0)

REDWOOD
TR (1.7)

CCC
BUNKHOUSE

TIE TRAIL (0.5)

PLUM
TR (1.7)

POLIPOLI
TR (0.6)

KAHUA RD TR (3.5)

HALEAKALA
RIDGE TR (1.6)

CAVE

TRAILS ...., (SEE MAP)
CAMPING ▲
CABINS ⬟
SHELTER ⌂
(MAP NOT TO SCALE)

POLIPOLI PARK
(Hiking Area No. 11)

Zone: Haleakala.

Rating: (See individual hikes.)

Features: Plums, redwoods, solitude, fresh and crisp air, birds and camping.

Permission: Tenting or cabin permits from Hawaii State Department of Natural Resources. (See "Maui's Campgrounds" and "Maui's Housekeeping Cabins" in the Introduction). Trail shelters are first come, first served. No fee and no permits are required to hike, to camp or to use the trail shelters.

Hiking Distance & Time: Consult individual hikes.

Driving Instructions:

   From Lahaina (50 miles, 2 hours) southeast on Route 30, right on Route 38, right on Route 36, right on Route 37 past Kula, left on Route 377 for 0.4 mile, right (10.5 miles) on Waipoli Road to end.

   From Wailuku (31 miles, 1 1/2 hours) east on Route 32, right on Route 36, then as above.

Introductory Notes: The Waipoli Road to Polipoli (lit., "mounds, bosom") follows a steep, winding, bumpy course. The initial portion of the road is paved, but the last three and one-half miles are not. Four-wheel-drive vehicles are recommended.

   Polipoli Park is an enjoyable hiking and camping area for the whole family. Although the road is difficult, it is well worth the effort for an overnight visit.   On weekends, usually in the early morning hours, you may be treated to some local hang-gliding enthusiasts "doing their thing" on the slopes of Haleakala.   These daring people, harnessed to kites that measure about 2 by 20 feet, take off around the 6,000-foot level for a fifteen-minute plus glide to the Forest Reserve entrance below.

   Polipoli Park is only a part of 12,000 acres that also comprise the Kula (lit., "open country") and

Kahikinui (lit., "great Tahiti") Forest Reserve on the upper west and south slopes of Haleakala Volcano. Native forests of koa, ohia and mamane have been largely destroyed since the 1800s by cattle, goats, fires and lumbering. During the 1920s a major reforestation and conservation project was begun by the state, and it was continued in the 1930s by the Civilian Conservation Corps. The result was the planting of hundreds of redwood, Monterey cypress, ash, sugi, cedar, and numerous types of pine.

Early mornings and evenings are usually clear, with fog, mist and light rain arriving later in the day. Annual rainfall is 20-40 inches, and the nights are generally cold-unexpected by visitors to Hawaii. Indeed, winter nights frequently have below-freezing temperatures. But don't be discouraged: at least those pesky mosquitoes are absent!

A number of birds may be found in the park along the trails. With the aid of a small booklet, *Hawaii's Birds*, published by the Hawaii Audubon Society, I have been able to identify the ring-necked pheasant (Phasianus colchicus torquatus), the chukar (Alectoris graeca), the California quail (Lophortyx californicus) with its distinctive head plume, the skylark (Alauda arvensis), and the ever-present mynah (Acridotheres tristis), which is probably the noisiest bird known to man. Indeed, the mynah, one of the most common birds on the island, is both intelligent and entertaining. One clue to recognizing it is that it walks as well as hops.

California Redwoods

ON THE TRAIL:

Redwood Trail, 1.7 miles, 1 hour, 900-foot gain (trail rating: hardy family).

The trail begins at the camping area at 6,200 feet and follows a circuitous route through stands of redwoods and other conifers to the 5,300-foot level. A state park cabin is located a couple of hundred yards from the camping area along the Redwood Trail. The view from the cabin is exciting and the sunsets can be very beautiful. Don't miss either. Markers identify many of the trees along the way, such as Mexican pine, tropical ash, Port Oxford cedar, sugi, and some junipers.

Aptly named, this trail is my favorite at Polipoli because of the hundreds of redwoods (Sequoia sempervirens) that were planted as part of the reforestation program in 1927. Since that time, these wondrous giants have grown to a height of about 90 feet, and some measure four feet or more in diameter at the base. The hike is a particular joy for those familiar with the California redwoods. To walk among these majestic trees, to delight in their fragrance, to feel the soft sod from accumulated needles underfoot, and to view the sun trying to force its way through their dense foliage is an overwhelming experience.

At trail's end, you are met by a generous garden of hydrangeas that seem to engulf the ranger's cabin, which is occupied only when the area is being serviced. However, flowers are not the main attraction here. Locals flock to this part of the park yearly to pick the Methley plum, which grow just below the cabin. The plums usually ripen in June, although they may be sweet by the end of May.

Tie Trail, 0.5 mile, 1/2 hour, 500-foot gain
(trail rating: family)

A trail shelter located at the junction of the Tie Trail and the Redwood Trail contains four bunks. The Tie Trail does what the name implies: it connects the Redwood Trail with the Plum Trail, descending 500 feet through stands of sugi, cedar and ash. The Tie Trail junction is 0.8 mile down the Redwood Trail. The Tie Trail joins the Plum Trail 0.6 mile south from the ranger's cabin.

Plum Trail, 1.7 miles, 1 1/2 hours
(trail rating: hardy family)

The trail begins at the ranger's cabin and the old Civilian Conservation Corps (CCC) bunkhouse and runs south until it meets the Haleakala Ridge Trail. The trailhead is a favorite spot to pick Methley plums during June and July. Both the ranger's cabin and the old CCC bunkhouse may be used for overnight shelter, but both are rough and weathered and do not provide drinking water or other facilities. Often, during late afternoon, the trail becomes shrouded by fog or mist, which makes for wet, damp, cool hiking. You should be prepared with rain gear.

Although the plums attract hikers, there are stands of ash, redwood and sugi trees as well. The trail terminates on a bluff overlooking the Ulupalakua ranch area of Maui.

Polipoli Trail, 0.6 mile, 1/2 hour
(trail rating: family)

This trail connects the camping area of the park with the Haleakala Ridge Trail. From the park it passes through rather dense stands of Monterey pine, red alder, cedar, pine and cypress, all of which emit delicious fragrances. Many fallen and cut trees provide an abundant supply of firewood for campers.

Haleakala Ridge Trail, 1.6 miles, 1 hour, 600-foot gain (Trail rating: family)

For a full panorama of the island, the Ridge Trail provides the best views, since it is not as heavily forested as other portions of the park. It begins at the terminal point of the Skyline Trail, at 6,550 feet, and follows the southwest rift of Haleakala to join with the Plum Trail at 5,950 feet.

Monterey pine, cypress, eucalyptus, blackwood, hybrid cypress and native grasses are identified by markers along the trail. At trail's end, be certain to investigate a small ten-by-twenty-foot dry cave located in a cinder cone and used as a trail shelter. An eight-by-ten-foot ledge in the cave provides a relatively comfortable king-sized bed. A spur trail to the cave is clearly marked and easy to follow.

Boundary Trail, 4.0 miles, 2 1/2 hours (trail rating: hardy family)

The Kula Forest Reserve boundary cattle guard on the Polipoli Road marks the trailhead for the Boundary Trail. This trail descends gradually along switchbacks to follow the northern boundary of the reserve to the ranger's cabin at the Redwood-Plum Trail Junction. Numerous points along the trail provide views of central Maui.

The trail crosses many gulches that abound in native scrub, ferns and grasses as well as stands of eucalyptus, Chinese fir, sugi, cedar and Monterey pine. About 1/2 mile below the cabin, fuchsia bushes proliferate to the point of obscuring the trail. As you pass through this garland of delicate red, lantern like flowers, a clearing encircled by eucalyptus trees appears across the fence.

Waiohuli Trail, 1.4 miles, 1 1/2 hours, 800-foot gain (trail rating: hardy family)

The rough Waiohuli (lit., "churning water")

Trail shelter

Trail begins on the Polipoli Road at 6,400 feet and goes straight down the mountainside to meet the Boundary Trail at the 5,600-foot level. The trail first passes rough, low, native scrub, young pine plantings and grasslands, and then wanders through older stands of cedar, redwood and ash.

The trail eventually joins the Boundary Trail, which is well-maintained and clearly identifiable. At this junction, another overnight shelter is conveniently located.

Waiakoa Trail, 7.0 miles, 5 hours, 1,800-foot gain (trail rating: strenuous)

The Upper Waiakoa Trailhead is opposite the Waiohuli Trailhead off the Polipoli Road. Carry sufficient water since no source can be found trailside. Initially, the trail ascends along switchbacks to the junction with the Mamane Trail, to a natural cave shelter and then turning northerly (left) and passing over rugged terrain consisting mostly of scrub vegetation. Look for pheasant and chukar partridge throughout the hike.

Outstanding views of central and West Maui are possible as you near the high point of the trail at 7,800 feet. Eucalyptus, mixed pine species, cedar, ash and native scrub dominate throughout interrupted by open places that offer a view of the summit of Haleakala, conspicuous by the white domes containing telescopes. Pukiawe, a common native bush in this forest, has tiny, evergreen leaves with reddish-white berries.

From there, the trail descends about 1,800 feet along a series of switchbacks to connect with the Waiakoa Loop Trail.

Waiakoa Loop Trail, 3 miles, 2 hours, 500-foot gain (trail rating: hardy family)

From the Hunter Checking Station, it's 3/4-mile to the Waiakoa (lit., "waters used by warrior") Loop Trailhead, which is a 3 mile Loop. From the game-checking station on the Polipoli Road follow the dirt road to the posted trailhead.

Once through the gate, the trail contours the hillside and after 100 yards it intersects the loop trail. Bearing right, the trail passes under a variety of trees, mostly black pine and eucalyptus. The latter are introduced trees planted for soil conservation.

When in bloom the native mamane tree offers a brilliant shower of bright yellow blossoms. The Hawaiians once used the hard wood for making spades and sled runners. Mamane trees are sometime mistaken for the wattle found throughout the trail. Wattle is an introduced tree with yellow blossoms, but usually much taller than the mamane.

After a mile or so, the trail emerges onto an area dominated by native and introduced scrub. At the 1 1/2-mile point, the trail begins to loop and descend over open, grassy swales and then forested places before beginning an ascent to complete the loop. fallen trees and large rocks throughout the hike afford places to pause to enjoy a snack, to inhale the fresh, crisp mountain air and to look for birdlife.

Mamane Trail, 1.2 miles, 1 hour
(trail rating: hardy family)

The Mamane Trail links the Skyline and Waiakoa trails and is used by hikers and bicyclists so be alert. The trail was reconstructed by volunteers under the direction of Na Ala Hele, the Hawaii State Trail and Access System. The trail passes through sparse native scrub brush and over cinder and rock.

Kahua Road, 3.5 miles, 3 hours
(trail rating: strenuous)

Used primarily by hunters, this road begins at Ballpark Junction where the Skyline Trail joins the road at 7,100 feet. It leads east on the contour through very rough lava country to the cinder cone called Kahua (lit., "jealousy"). Even a four-wheeled drive vehicle has difficulty traversing this road. An overnight cabin here is maintained by the state, and arrangements can be made in Wailuku for its use. It accommodates four people and has water. The primary attraction is the view of the east side and the rugged coastline. On clear days it is possible to see across Kahukinui to the Kaupo Gap. This is a very hot and difficult hike.

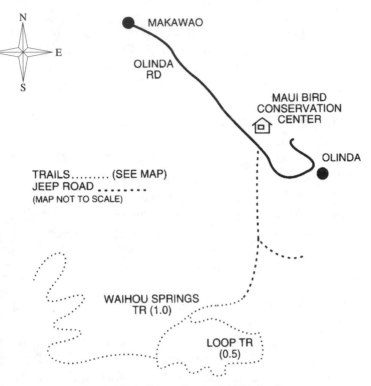

WAIHOU SPRINGS
(Hiking Area No. 12)

Zone: Haleakala.

Rating: Family.

Features: Forest hike.

Permission: None.

Hiking Distance & Time: 1.5 miles (main trail and loop trail), 1 1/2 hours.

Driving Instructions:

From Lahaina (39 Miles, 1 hour) southeast on Route 30, right on Route 38, right on Route

36, right on Route 37, left on Route 365 to Makawao Town, right on Olinda Road for 4.7 miles to trailhead on the right.

From Wailuku (17 miles 1/2 hour) east on Route 32, right on Route 36 then as above.

Introductory Notes: Waihou (Lit., "new water") Springs Trail was adopted in 1994 by the Sierra Club, Maui Group whose volunteer members regularly maintain the trial. This is a delightful family hike in Maui's cool upcountry.

On the Trail: The trailhead is clearly posted on the right side of Olinda Road. The trail follows an unpaved road that parallels a state experimental forest on the left containing mostly loblolly pine. The plantings in the 1920s was an attempt to restore watershed.

After 0.2-mile, the road swings left and our trail goes straight under a canopy of trees and

Taro

continues for about 200 yards to a junction. Here, the loop trail goes left and up an easy grade while the main trail swings right for 100 yards to another junction where the main trail makes a right turn and the loop trail goes straight. A variety of tall trees including eucalyptus and mountain ash shade the trail throughout.

The main trail descends to a tableland where Girl Scout Troop 792 planted eight native koa trees in 1996. On a recent visit, I observed that only six were living. Several breaks in the forest along this portion of the trail offer views of the West Maui Mountains. From the flat land, the trail goes right, narrows and descends abruptly about one-fourth mile to the bottom of the gulch. Keep a watchful eye on children throughout this part of the trail.

Typically, the springs at the bottom of the gulch are dry. From writings at the turn of the century, we learn that the springs were once a major source of water providing an average of 8,000 gallons of water a day for the ranchers and residents in the Olinda area. Several tunnels and intakes which were dug by hand are visible on the walls above the springs. Except during periods of heavy rainfall, the springs are dry primarily because the forest land above was denuded earlier this century. Recent reforestation programs are an effort to restore the watershed.

Return on the main trail to the junction with the Loop Trail. It's an easy stroll through a wooded area similar to that found on the main trail.

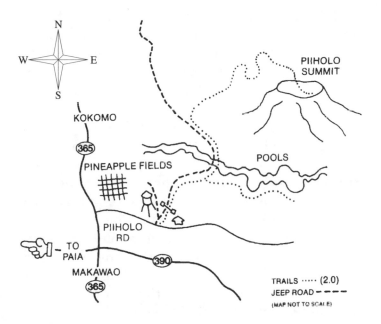

PIIHOLO HILL
(Hiking Area No. 13)

Zone: Haleakala.

Rating: Hardy family.

Features: Views, gulches, pasture land, swimming, common and strawberry guavas.

Permission: Haleakala Ranch Co. Telephone 572-7326. (Organized groups only).

Hiking Distance & Time: 2 miles, 1 hour, 560 foot gain.

Driving Instructions:

From Lahaina (35 miles, 1 hour) southeast

on Route 30, right on Route 38, right on Route 36, right on Route 37, left on Route 365 through Makawao for 0.2 mile, right on Piiholo Road for 0.5 mile to a water tank on the left. Park on the shoulder of the road. Do not park on pineapple road.

From Wailuku (16 miles, 1/2 hour) east on Route 32, right on Route 36, then as above.

Introductory Notes: Piiholo (lit., "going up") is a rewarding hike, particularly if you have a fondness for common and strawberry guavas. Most of the trail passes guava-laden trees, with strawberry guavas to be found at the trail's end at the summit. Follow the gulch trail after your hike and enjoy a swim in the generous pools formed by the mountain stream.

CAUTION: Do not hike on the south side of Piiholo. It is extremely precipitous, with vertical cliffs up to 500 feet high

On the Trail: Climb over the gate behind the water tower and follow the jeep road that descends right to the gulch below. The route for the ascent of Piiholo swings left at the bottom of the gulch and follows an overgrown jeep road across the stream and up the northeast side of the mountain. It is necessary to climb over a gate to continue north. A spur road swings right to follow the south side of the gulch. Again, do not proceed along the south side, for it is extremely precipitous and dangerous. By now, you should be sampling the yellow, lemon-sized guavas. I have found some relatively sweet guavas on the hike. Be selective and choose those that are soft to the touch.

As the jeep road begins to cross the pasture land, about 0.3 mile from the gate, continue your ascent by cutting across the cattle paths on the northwest side of Piiholo. There is no clearly defined trail. All's well as long as you are in open pasture land and you continue along the northwest side. A jeep road does descend for 1/2 mile from the summit, running from the north to the east side. Continue your ascent to the eucalyptus-tree line, and you are certain to run into the jeep road that leads to the summit. (The grazing cattle are not aggressive and probably will run away as you approach).

From the summit, the panorama of the coastline from Haiku in the north, across central Maui, to Kihei on the south shore is overwhelming. In addition, you overlook one of the most beautiful views of the upcountry area, with its pineapple fields, small farms and rural residences. As always, Haleakala appears majestic, overlooking its creation.

Strawberry guavas are abundant around the summit. The deep red fruits are the sweetest, providing a tasty supplement to your lunch.

Your descent is easy, particularly if you are anticipating a refreshing swim in a sparkling fresh water pool. You'll probably hear joyful voices coming from local children who frequent the pools. Hike along the trail that follows the gulch and choose a pool that suits you. (Do not dive or jump into a pool until you have checked for submerged rocks).

Where's the trail?

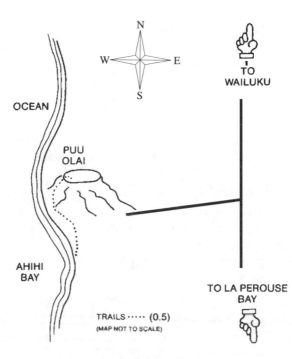

TRAILS ····· (0.5)
(MAP NOT TO SCALE)

PUU OLAI
(Hiking Area No. 14)

Zone: South.

Rating: Family.

Features: One of Maui's best beaches, views of Lanai, Molokini, Kahoolawe and upcountry, swimming, nude sunbathing, tide pools, snorkeling, volcanic formations.

Permission: None.

Hiking Distance & Time: 0.5 mile, 1/2 hour, 360 foot gain.

Driving Instructions:

From Lahaina (32 miles, 1 1/4 hours) southeast on Route 30, then right on Route 31 to Makena Beach. Puu Olai is a conspicuous promontory on the shoreline. Turn right to the parking lot.

From Wailuku (21 miles, 3/4 hour) south on Route 30, left on Route 31, then as above.

Introductory Notes: Puu Olai (lit., "earthquake hill") is known locally as "round mountain," and the beach is known as "Big Beach." The hill is conspicuous two miles after you pass Makena Landing. The Ahihi (lit., "calm, clear") Bay area was once called "hippie town" due to the many transients who took to homesteading among the kiawe trees and on the beach in their makeshift plastic and some times wood shacks. Recently, a paved road and parking lot has been

Puu Olai

constructed to allow easy access. CAUTION: DO NOT leave valuables in your vehicle, and protect them on the beach.

The summit of Puu Olai may be approached from the north or south. The southern approach is easier and takes you to a point on the summit for the best views.

Boots and long pants are recommended if you plan to walk around the summit or to hike to the other peaks, for the brush is very dense.

On the Trail: The trail begins at the north end of Ahihi Beach, although from a distance it appears as though the cliff extends to the water line. From here, it's straight up - 360 feet - along a ridge to the summit. The view from the summit is a photographer's delight. The white sandy beach of Ahihi Bay lies below, and the uninhabited islands of Molokini and Kahoolawe are offshore. The island of Lanai is in the distant west.

It is possible to cross over to the other peaks and descend the steeper north side of the mountain. If you choose to do so, you can return to Ahihi Bay on the road around the east side. The beach "trail" follows the beach around the west side.

"Little Beach," — a popular nude swimming beach — north of "Big Beach" is separated by a low wall of lava. It is necessary to climb over the lava to reach the beach. For many, it's worth the effort!

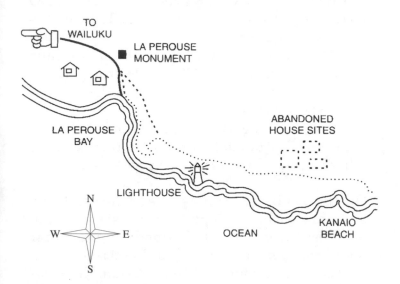

TO
WAILUKU
LA PEROUSE
MONUMENT
LA PEROUSE
BAY
ABANDONED
HOUSE SITES
LIGHTHOUSE
N
W   E
S
OCEAN
KANAIO
BEACH

TRAIL .... (5.5 MI)
JEEP ROAD ....
(MAP NOT TO SCALE)

KING'S HIGHWAY
HOAPILI TRAIL
(Hoapili Trail)
(Hiking Area No. 15)

Zone: South.

Rating: Difficult.

Features: Trail/road constructed by early Hawaiians, Polynesian village ruins, lava flows, snorkeling, fishing.

Permission: None.

Hiking Distance & Time: 5.5 miles, 3 hours.

Driving Instructions:

From Lahaina (35 miles, 1 1/2 hours) southeast on Route 30,then right on Route 31. The paved road ends at the La Perouse monument on the left side of the road. Turn right past the monument and park by the shoreline.

From Wailuku (24 miles, 1 hour) south on Route 30, left on Route 31, then as above.

Introductory Notes: La Perouse Bay was named after the French explorer who anchored there in 1786, met with the natives, and sailed away to mysteriously disappear at sea. He described his first impression of the bay as ". . . a dismal coast, where torrents of lava had formerly flowed." As a student of the French enlightenment and, therefore, a humanitarian, La Perouse regarded it his duty to help the people he visited. He was unlike most explorers of his time whose common practice was to claim new lands in the name of their benefactor, king or country. La Perouse accordingly wrote in his journal, "Although the French were the first in these latest times to land on Maui, I did not think it was my right to take possession of it in the name of the King. The customs of Europeans in this respect are completely ridiculous."

Another foreign touch in the area is the conspicuous cactus along the road that was introduced by some homesick Latin American cowboys.

On the Trail: The trail is well-defined but very rough, due to the rocky, volcanic underfooting. You will be hiking across the most recent lava flow (circa 1750) on Maui, and hiking to Kanaio Beach. You have the choice of following the "King's Highway" which is 100 yards up from the beach and which goes straight across the lava flows or of walking the shoreline on trails and jeep roads made by local fishermen who you'll likely see casting from the shore and lava rock promontories. Either way, you will be walking east and passing through many former home sites, heiaus, wells and towers that constituted a rather large Polynesian village. Many of the sites are conspicuous by their prominent stone

Hoapili Trail

walls; others require some investigation and imagination to identify. The "highway" was constructed to allow the tax collector to get to the homesteads in the area.

At the far end of La Perouse Bay, about one mile from the trailhead, is one of the best snorkeling spots on this side of the island. You'll find a heavily foliated beach front with kiawe trees and a sand/lava shoreline with a lava wall extending into the water. You'll likely see boats anchored here and snorkelers in the bay. This is the best place on this hike to snorkel and lunch. The bay and adjacent places contain a large variety of reef fish and tidepools with an abundance of marine life.

From here, you must make your way across very rough lava or go inland about 100 yards and hike on the "King's Highway." You will see a lighthouse (in fact, a coastal light beacon) at the 2-mile point on the tip of Cape Hanamanioa. A spur trail (.75-mile) leads to the Cape.

The trail/highway continues for several more miles. Puu Pimoe, a 500-foot cinder cone, stands about 3 miles inland and is the place from which the lava underfoot spewed in the 1750s. The broad stretch of coastline is known as Kanaio Beach where you'll find numerous small coves with pebble or coral beaches.

After five miles the trail passes onto private land.

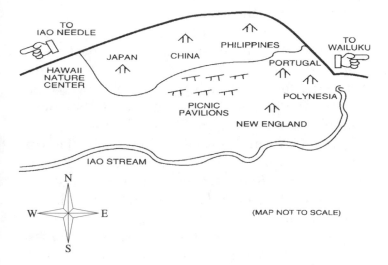

KAPANIWAI HERITAGE PARK
(Hiking Area No.16)

Zone: Central.
Rating: Family
Features: Picnic grounds, cultural displays, swimming.
Permission: None
Hiking Distance & Time: 0.3 mile, 15 minutes.
Driving Instructions:

From Lahaina (23 miles, 1 hour) southeast on Route 30 to Wailuku, left on Route 32 to Kepaniwai County Park (posted on left).

From Wailuku (2 miles, 5 minutes) See above instructions.

Introductory Notes: Kepaniwai's (Lit., "the water dam") name is attributed to a fierce battle that was fought here in 1790. Kamehameha The Great defeated Maui forces in a battle so bloody that Iao Stream become dammed with corpses.

The park contains numerous sheltered picnic tables, a swimming pool (open only in the summer) and a stream which sometime contains sufficient water in which to soak your feet.

On the Trail: From the parking lot you can determine your route to visit the Japanese Teahouse, Chinese Pagoda, Philippines house, Portuguese house and outdoor oven, New England salt box house and Polynesia grass house. Each structure represents a prominent Maui ethnic group who in cooperation with Maui County has built and maintains their respective building.

Numerous sheltered picnic tables provide a comfortable lunch spot. Some visitors walk to Iao Stream below the parking lot to snack and splash in the stream. It's pleasurable to sit by the stream and to view the heavily foliated, near vertical walls of the valley. The Nature Center located west of the parking area offers a variety of activities for children.

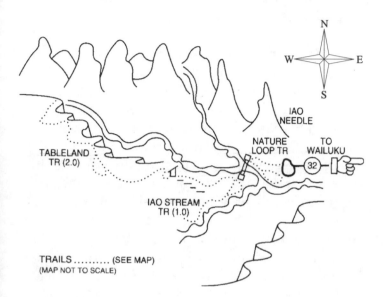

IAO VALLEY
(Hiking Area No. 17)

Zone: Central.

Rating: Consult individual hikes.

Features: Strawberry and common guavas, swimming, native flora, and views of central Maui, Iao Valley and Iao Needle.

Permission: Wailuku Agribusiness, Tel.244-9570 for permit to hike beyond posted "No Trespassing" signs.

Hiking Distance & Time: See individual hikes.

Driving Instructions:

From Lahaina (24 miles, 1 hour) southeast on Route 30 to Wailuku, left on Route 32 to end.

FromWailuku (3 miles, 1/4 hour) west on Route 32 to end.

Introductory Notes: Few people dispute that Iao (lit., "valley of dawning inspiration") Valley is one of the most beautiful valleys on Maui. It has long been favorite of locals and tourists, who come to see the Iao Needle, the John Kennedy Profile, and the splendid tropical gardens and streams.

Iao Valley Trailheads

The area surrounding the state park is owned by Wailuku Agribusiness; however, trails and paths have been "established" by locals and visitors and are used by securing permission. Use extreme caution when hiking off the trail in the stream, for the mossy rocks are treacherous. I have lost count of the twisted ankles and bruised knees I have received there, not to mention the times I have fallen into the stream.

The whole family can enjoy Iao. There are casual family walks as well as more difficult hikes to challenge the adventurer. However, do not hike the streams when it is raining in the higher areas because of the possibility of flash flooding. Each year the streams are altered considerably by the seasonal rains and resulting floods; therefore, pools, small waterfalls and other such features mentioned here may no longer exist. You can expect, however, that other pools and waterfalls will have been created.

Nature Loop, 100 yards (trail rating: family).

ON THE TRAIL: The shortest, but pleasurable walk begins just before the bridge and bears left, descending to a small garden. A local Hawaiian group intends to plan a garden containing only native plants, which will be identified.

Iao Needle

Tableland Trail, 2 miles, 1 1/2 hours, 500-foot gain (trail rating: hardy family).

ON THE TRAIL: (Permit required) From the parking lot at the end of the road, cross the bridge and follow the paved walk to the lookout shelter. The trail to the tableland begins behind the shelter. The first 1/2 mile is relatively steep, with a gain of 500 feet. At this point, the Needle is all but indistinguishable as you view it's west side across Kinihapai Stream. As you continue, watch for a short trail on the left that leads to the top of the ridge. Follow this spur trail and continue along the razorback for a spectacular view of Iao Valley and Wailuku. The razorback detour then rejoins the Tableland Trail, which is level to the tableland. Between August and October, strawberry guavas flourish along the trail. This red, walnut-sized fruit may be eaten whole or after removing the small seeds insides. Sample them, but for the most succulent selections do your picking on the tableland.

In addition to the profuse guavas, ti plants and ferns abound in this area. As you approach the tableland, the strawberry guavas become more abundant. The tableland is identified by the tall, chest-high grass on a large flat area ringed by guava trees. Pick, eat and enjoy the varieties of guavas. The common guavas may be eaten whole, although some prefer to eat the inner portion, which is sweeter without the skin.

Local people complain that it is no longer possible to find truly sweet guavas like those they ate when they were young; however, to a visitor these fruits are delicious.

A tasty drink may be concocted from the guavas you bring back from your hikes if you have a blender. Wash the whole guava and place in the blender. Add one cup of water. Reduce by blending to a syrup, and strain. Mix this syrup with your favorite base (orange, grapefruit, passion fruit) to taste. Serve with ice or after chilling.

The trail passes straight through the tableland and into moderately heavy growth and swings right on a winding, ascending course for about 0.5-mile to a marvelous viewpoint - when it's not cloudy - from which you can view the dramatic pali (cliffs) here. USE CAUTION on the last 100 yards of the trail because it is steep, muddy, and overgrown. Usually, several waterfalls can be sighted from trail's end.

Iao Stream Trail, 1 mile, 1/2 hour
(trail rating: family).

ON THE TRAIL: (Permit required) From the parking lot, cross over the bridge and turn down the walk to the stream below for a swim. There are a number of sizable pools. You'll probably share the pools with local children who frequent the area; better yet, find your own private pool.

A well-defined trail extends along the stream

and abruptly ends at a large pool. BE CAU-
TIOUS if you choose to swim. The rocks, when
wet, are very slippery. It's a pleasant place to
snack, to dangle your feet in the water and to
enjoy the lush foliage. White and yellow ginger
surround the pool and common guavas hang from
above sometime falling on the rocks and into the
pool to sweeten the water.

Sugar cane - Hawaiian candy bars

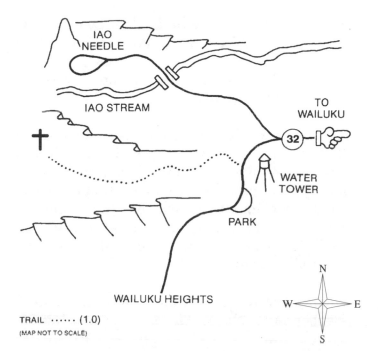

IAO
NEEDLE

IAO STREAM

TO
WAILUKU

32

WATER
TOWER

PARK

WAILUKU HEIGHTS

TRAIL ······ (1.0)
(MAP NOT TO SCALE)

N
W———E
S

CROSS ABOVE WAILUKU
(Hiking Area No. 18)

Zone: Central.

Rating: Strenuous.

Features: Views of Iao Valley and central Maui.

Permission: Wailuku Agribusiness, Telephone 244-9570.

Hiking Distance & Time: 1 mile, 1 hour, 1,000-foot gain.

Driving Instructions:

From Lahaina (23 miles, 1 hour) southeast on Route 30 to Wailuku, left on Route 32, bear

left at junction to Wailuku Heights. Look for telephone pole No. 5 on right. Park in turnout on
left.

From Wailuku (2 miles, 1/4 hour) west on
Route 32, then as above.

Introductory Notes: In 1956 students from
St. Anthony High School in Wailuku placed a
cross above the town. Since then, they have re-
placed the original cross with one that can with-
stand the elements. Each year the seniors at
the school, as part of an annual graduation
project, hike to the cross for general repairs and
maintenance work.

On the Trail: The trailhead is to the right of
telephone pole No. 5. This is a strenuous but enjoyable hike. The views into Iao Valley are
breathtaking. There are numerous overlooks
before reaching the cross that offer views and a
chance to catch your breath.

If you have any energy remaining when you
reach the cross, it is worth the extra effort to
continue up Kapilau (lit., "sprinkle of rain on
leaves") Ridge for spectacular views into Iao Valley. On a clear day, waterfalls and cascades are
visible in the recess of Iao. USE EXTREME
CAUTION, for the spine of the ridge narrows to
a few feet at point, with steep vertical cliffs on
each side.

It is easy to become preoccupied with Iao Valley, but there are also unobstructed views of central Maui and a generous panorama of the island.

Kanaha Pond

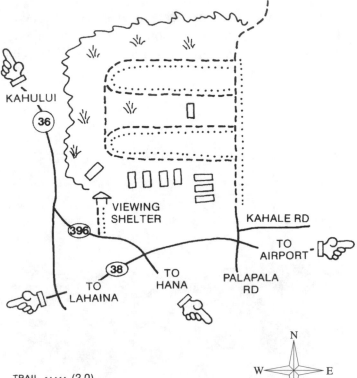

KAHULUI

VIEWING
SHELTER

KAHALE RD

TO
AIRPORT

TO
HANA

PALAPALA
RD

TO
LAHAINA

TRAIL ····· (2.0)
JEEP ROAD ----
(MAP NOT TO SCALE)

N
W——E
S

KANAHA BIRD SANCTUARY
(Hiking Area No. 19)
Open April-August.

Zone: Central.

Rating: Family.

Features: Birds - rare Hawaiian stilt and Hawaiian coot; World War II munitions bunkers.

Permission: Department of Natural Resources, Division of Forestry, Tel., 984-8100 for permit.

Hiking Distance & Time: 2 miles, 1 hour.
Driving Instructions:

From Lahaina (20 miles, 3/4 hour) southeast
on Route 30, right on Route 38 to Palapala Road
(opposite Department of Water Supply building),
turn left and park at entrance.

From Wailuku (2 miles, 1/4 hour) east on
Route 32, right on Route 36, left on Airport Road,
then as above.

Introductory Notes: The Division of Forestry
requires written permits to hike on the sanctuary that is not open during breeding season —
September-March. There is no fee. No permit is
required to visit the viewing shelter off Route
396.

On the Trail: There are two loop roads of one
mile each which may be taken at a leisurely pace.
Each road provides close-up views of the birds.
Binoculars heighten one's pleasure, but are not
essential. The birds are quite close to the road
and do not seem to be affected by visitors.

Interesting features of the hike are the many
World War II munitions bunkers along the road.
Some bunkers are abandoned and are readily
available for inspection, while others are locked
and used by local businesses for storage.

Two birds deserve special note. One is the
Hawaiian stilt (Himantopus knudseni), or aeo
(lit., "one who walks on stilts"). The stilt is eas-

ily recognized. It measures just over 16 inches
and has long, thin, pink legs, a blue-black back,
and a pure white breast. It nests and feeds in
the mud flats of the lagoon. Although the stilt is
on the endangered-species list, it is doing well
at Kanaha (lit., "forty") Pond, according to local
wardens.

Hawaiian coots (Fulica americana alae), or
keokeos (lit., "white"), are playful birds that
chase one another. They have a white bill, an
ivory-white frontal shield, and slate-colored
plumage on their back and under parts. They
nest in a floating structure of reeds or other vegetation, sometimes three feet thick.

Fruit picking on the trail

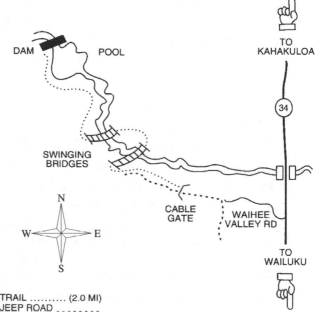

DAM   POOL

TO KAHAKULOA

34

SWINGING BRIDGES

N
W E
S

CABLE GATE

WAIHEE VALLEY RD

TO WAILUKU

TRAIL .... (2.0 MI)
JEEP ROAD ....
(MAP NOT TO SCALE)

WAIHEE VALLEY
(Hiking Area No. 20)

Zone: Central.

Rating: Hardy Family.

Features: Swimming, waterfalls, views, fruits.

Permission: Maui Agribusiness, Tel. 244-9570 for written permit.

Hiking Distance & Time: 2 miles, 1 1/2 hours.

Driving Instructions:

From Lahaina (31 miles, 1 1/4 hours) southeast on Route 30 to Wailuku, right on Route 32, left on Route 34 (Kahului Beach Road), right on

Route 34 through Waihee, left on Waihee Road
0.7 mile from Waihee School, follow paved road
for 0.5 mile to end, and bear right on unpaved
road for 0.2 mile to cable gate. Park your car on
the shoulder outside the gate even if the cable is
unlocked when you arrive, it may not be when
you return.

From Wailuku (10 miles, 1/2 hour) east on
Route 32, left on Route 34, then as above.

Introductory Notes: Waihee (lit., "slippery water") Valley is one of the easiest valley hikes on
the island, and it is one of the prettiest valleys
on the island, with narrow canyon and steep vertical walls from which water cascades and falls.
The terrain is relatively level for the whole distance. Since it is a watershed area, hikers should
not hike beyond the dam.

On the Trail: From your car, walk up the road
and bear right. The first mile of the hike is on a
maintenance road that follows the stream (right)
and an irrigation channel (left). Look for guava
trees and thimbleberries along the trail. The ginger is particularly abundant, and conspicuous by
its fragrant aroma. There are torch ginger, with
its long, bamboo-like stalk and red blossom, and
yellow ginger, which is more fragrant.

Ti (Cordyline terminalis) plants are also
abundant. They should be familiar to all visitors who have seen a hula show. The long, narrow leaves are used to make hula skirts, and have

also been used by Hawaiians to make thatch, raincoats, sandals, plates to serve food, and wrappers for food.

As the trail levels, there are views into the valley and east to the ocean. The stream is usually dry up to the point of the water intake. After one mile, two successive swinging bridges cross the stream bed. After crossing the second bridge, be on the lookout for mountain apple trees (eugenia malaccensis) alongside the trail. I could find only a couple of these trees, which bear a small, deep-crimson fruit with a pure-white pulp and a large, round seed. It is much sought after by locals, who know the best places and best trees.

Be careful here, particularly with children, because after the bridges the trail climbs above the stream along the canyon wall. Below the ridge, an elaborate irrigation system is designed to catch the stream water and to channel it via a system of ditches. This is a good opportunity to examine the system up close. Upstream about 200 yards is a second dam and water-intake system. This is the end of the trail. From here, you are able to view the waterfalls in the back of the canyon as well as the steep vertical walls. Below the dam, large pools provide a cool swim or a refreshing splash.

It is possible to continue into the canyon by following the stream, but the going is rough and wet. If it is raining in the canyon, there is also the danger of flash flooding.

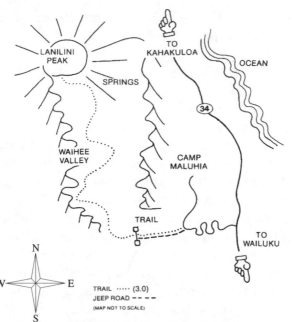

WAIHEE RIDGE
(Hiking Area No. 21)

Zone: Central.
Rating: Strenuous.
Features: Views of Waihee Canyon and Valley, Central Maui, the north side.
Permission: None.
Hiking Distance & Time: 3.0 miles, 2 hours, 1,500 foot gain.
Driving Instructions:

From Lahaina (32 miles, 1 1/4 hour) southeast on Route 30 to Wailuku, right on Route 32, left on Route 34, (Kahului Beach Road) through Waihee. Turn left on road posted "Camp

Maluhia" and drive 0.8 mile to the trailhead a short distance before the camp.

From Wailuku (11 miles, 1/2 hour) east on Route 32, left on Route 34, then as above.

Introductory Notes: The Waihee (lit., "slippery water") Ridge trail and area are under the management of the Hawaii State Department of Land and Natural Resources and are regularly maintained.

On the Trail: From the parking area, pass through a turnstile and cross the pasture and

Waihee Ridge Trailhead

ascend to the trees above. You may be surprised by grazing cattle in the heavy brush along the road. Relatively sweet common and strawberry guava abound along the trail. Shortly, a gate across the road marks the border of forest-reserve land. If the gate is locked, passage is provided a few feet to the right of the gate. In a few hundred feet the road ends and a foot trail begins. It turns right and climbs the ridge through an area of grass, ferns and trees.

The trail is marked every 1/4 mile. There are a number of overlooks into Waihee Canyon and to the north into Makamakaole (lit., "not without intimate friends") Gulch. At the 0.7 mile point and beyond for a distance, there are superb views of the valley. Thereafter, the trail switchbacks and ascends the narrow ridge that is heavily foliated, wet, muddy, and in places quite steep so that it is necessary to use the trees and bushes for support. After two miles, the trail reaches a flat, grassy tableland that may or may not be passable if it is too wet and boggy.

Be on the lookout for edible thimbleberries (Rubus rosaefolius), which grow profusely in this area. These red berries grow on a small bush with white flowers.

From the tableland, it is less than a mile to Lanilili (lit., "small heaven") Peak and breathtaking views of the north side of the island and of the surrounding valleys. Conveniently, a picnic table is on the summit.

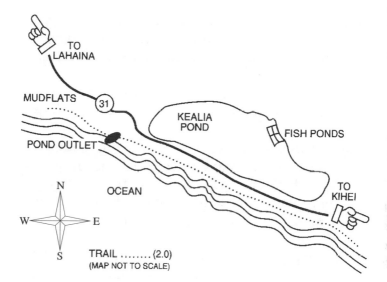

TO
LAHAINA

MUDFLATS (31)

KEALIA
POND

FISH PONDS

POND OUTLET

N

OCEAN

TO
KIHEI

W——E

S

TRAIL ....(2.0)
(MAP NOT TO SCALE)

KEALIA POND NATIONAL WILDLIFE REFUGE

(Hiking Area No. 22)

Zone: West.

Rating: Family.

Features: Coastal hike, turtles, whales, native and introduced fauna and swimming.

Permission: None.

Hiking Distance & Time: 2 miles, 1 hour.

Driving Instructions:

From Lahaina (20 miles, 1/2 hour) Southeast on Route 30, turn right on Route 31 and drive

to the south end of Kealia Pond National Wildlife Refuge to their office located in the first
cluster of buildings on the right at 101 North
Kihei Road.

From Wailuku (8 miles, 1/4 hour) South on
Route 30, turn left on Route 31, then as above.

Introductory Notes: Millions of acres of wetlands have been paved over for civic "improve-
ments." By some estimates, less than half of the
original wetlands nationwide remain intact. In
Hawaii, the picture is even more bleak, with less
than 10 percent of wetlands remaining. Today,
wetlands are recognized as an important habi-
tant for a wide variety of birds and other wildlife. Some like Kealia Pond have won protection
as federal refuges. To best appreciate the birds
found here, carry binoculars and a copy of
Hawaii's Birds, published by the Hawaii
Audubon Society.

On the Trail: Before hiking, visit the Refuge
office where considerable free information is
available. Walk out to the ocean and turn north
(right) paralleling the highway. This stretch of
beach is popular with walkers, runners, fishermen, swimmers and divers. Out to sea, you might
spot turtles or, from November to April, humpback whales.

On an early morning walk between July and
December, you may find the tracks of a honu'ea
or hawksbill turtle. If you spot a hawksbill,

you're one of the lucky few. Experts estimate there are only a couple of dozen in the state. An adult can reach 200 pounds and is distinguished from the larger green turtle by it long, narrow beak. The hawksbill is threatened at almost every turn; cats, dogs and mongooses eat its eggs and hatchlings; at sea, adult turtles become entangled in or ingest plastic debris, or fall prey to sharks. In the past few years, two egg-bearing females, perhaps disoriented by headlights, were hit an killed while crossing Route 31 in search of a nesting site.

The pond on the north side of the road encompasses more than 250 acres when full. To protect the wildlife, the entrance on the north side of the highway is closed. But birds can be observed from atop the roadside berm. If you choose to cross the highway, watch out for fast-moving traffic.

The pond outlet and mud flats between1.4-mile and the two-mile point is the best place to observe wildlife. Numerous migratory birds, waterfowl and shore birds frequent these wetlands depending on the water level and season. The mud flats are usually inundated by winter rains from January to April. This allows the birds to find invertebrates and small fish in the shallow water.

In addition to night herons, two native Hawaiian waterbirds, the alae ke'oke'o (Fulica americana alai) or Hawaiian coot and the ae'o (Himantopus mexicanus knudseni) or black-necked stilt, frequent the pond. The coot is solid gray/black with a white bill and bulbous frontal shield. They rarely fly and will build nests from aquatic vegetation, which they will vigorously defend.

Bird experts estimate the state's population of black-necked stilts at 1200. Although on the endangered species list, stilts commonly occupy the pond's shallows and mud flats, probing for fish, insects and crabs. This tall, slender bird is conspicuous with its thin, chopstick-sized pink legs, long, thin black bill and black back and white breast. A timid bird, the stilt will fly away when it feels threatened. So walk slowly and quietly if you want to see it up close.

Occasionally, ospreys, which feed solely on fish, visit Kealia Pond. Large, glossy-brown birds with white underparts and a brown band across the breast, ospreys, also known as fish hawks, are excellent divers.

Plans call for a 4400-foot boardwalk along the south side of the refuge extending from the pond's outlet west along the sand dunes and mud flats. The project includes a parking area, a kiosk, outdoor classroom, interpretive displays and a bridge over the pond outlet. The boardwalk, designed to protect native wildlife and the integrity of the environment, will parallel the shoreline about 50 yards inland. It will also allow the public to enjoy this important refuge.

Although short, this hike will leave a lasting impression.

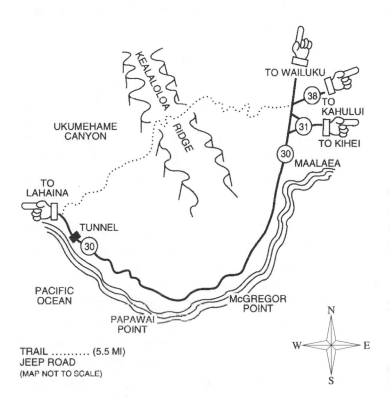

TRAIL .... (5.5 MI)
JEEP ROAD
(MAP NOT TO SCALE)

LAHAINA PALI
(Hiking Area No. 23)

Zone: West.

Rating: Strenuous.

Features: Views of Central Maui, Kihei, Haleakala, Molokini, Kahoolawe, Lanai, Hawaii.

Permission: None

Hiking Distance & Time: 5.5 miles, 3 hours, 1,600-foot gain/loss.

Driving Instructions:

From Lahaina (11 miles, 1/2 hour to westside trailhead)southeast on Route 30 to 11-mile marker and parking lot on the left side of the road.

From Wailuku (6 miles, 1/4 hour to eastside trailhead) south on Route 30 to 5-mile marker just past junction with Route 38. Cross over a white bridge and turn right to posted trailhead.

Introductory Notes: Originally constructed in 1840, the Lahaina Pali Trail fell into disrepair with the construction of a carriage road and later the present highway along the coast. Then in 1992, Na Ala Hele, (Lit., trails to go") a state-wide organization under the State Department of Land and Natural Resources surveyed, cleared and brushed the trail aided by hundreds of volunteers. The trail was dedicated in June, 1993.

I recommend that you begin hiking from the Maalaea (east side) Trailhead. This is the steeper part of the trail, but, if you begin hiking in the morning, the sun will be at your back. If you have two vehicles, leave one at the opposite trailhead. This is a hot hike with infrequent shade. Two quarts of water per person and sound hiking boots are recommended. Rocks and exposed tree roots are underfoot and are a hazard through-out the trail.

On the Trail: From the trailhead, walk on the dirt road with your back to the highway directly toward the base of the mountain. The road turns left and goes about 150 yards to a posted parking area and a trail sign which directs you off the road and onto a footpath shaded by large kiawe (Prosopis pallida) trees, a common tree found on the islands whose thorns seem to find their way into feet and legs. Its branches are long, slender and flexible, while the flowers are pale yellow and tiny. The bark contains tannin and a gum that is valuable in making varnish and glue. The wood is a source not only of fuel and lumber but also of honey, medicine and fodder, which is produced from its bean like yellow pods containing 25% grape sugar.

The trail begins a steady climb up the east side toward Kealaloloa Ridge. Look on both sides of the trail for abandoned concrete water wells and for concrete platforms that held large guns. The site was a military post constructed during WW II as a part of the island's defense system. Several metal posts and rolls of barbed wire mark the military boundary at the half-mile mark.

Shortly thereafter, the trail emerges from the canopy provided by the kiawe trees and follows a steeper, serpentine course. You're likely to find glass fragments and even bottles scattered on the trail and trailside. You're asked to inspect them if you choose, but to leave them where found. They may be significant artifacts which may be collected and studied at some future date. The trail curbing throughout the hike is thought to be from the original trail construction. Some of it is in good condition and an example of dry wall construction still commonly employed in Hawaii.

After the first mile, the trail becomes increasingly steeper but the views improve with every step. To the east, Kahului, the airport, sugar and pineapple fields comprise the neck portion of Maui with Haleakala, the house of the sun, overlooking its creation in the distance.

Low scrub and ground cover dominate throughout the next few miles. Puakala (Argemone glauca) is a white, prickly poppy related to the common North American species. Lantana (Lantana camara) is a popular flower that blooms almost continuously. Its flowers vary in color from yellow to orange to pink or red. Another flower, the ilima (Sida fallax) has bright flowers ranging in color from yellow to rich orange to dull red.

Several ironwood trees (Casuarina equisetifolia) are conspicuous on the ridge line to the west which is approximately the midpoint and the highest point (1,600 feet) on the trail. From this vista, you might be able to distinguish Hawaii, "the Big Island" to the right of Haleakala. To the south, lies Kihei, Maui's "Gold Coast," and offshore, the islands of Molokini, Kahoolawe and Lanai. As a bonus, between November and March, migratory humpback whales can be spotted in the waters below where they come to mate or to give birth.

From the ridge, the trail begins a gentle descent passing over a jeep road that goes north up the ridge and continuing on to the Olowalu Trailhead a few miles distant. More kiawe trees and vegetation provide some shade for the balance of the hike. State officials believe that abandoned house sites are scattered along this side of the ridge, but further studies need to be made. If you explore off the trail do not disturb or remove rocks. Look for letters chiseled on large rocks below the ridge. Most of them are letters in the paniolo (cowboy) style with bars at the bottom of the letter. Some of the writing may be decades old while others are more recent. It is believed that students passing through over the years may have used the rocks to practice their lettering.

The foot trail joins the old Lahaina carriage trail about 100 yards from the Olowalu Trailhead and the main highway. Follow the road a short distance to a foot path on the left that descends a stone stairway to the trailhead and a parking lot. A long, white sand beach and several shady picnic spots are just across the highway. It's also a good swimming and snorkeling beach.

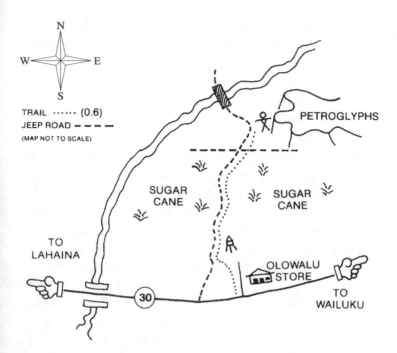

OLOWALU VALLEY
PETROGLYPHS
(Hiking Area No. 24)

Zone: West.

Rating: Family.

Features: Petroglyphs.

Permission: Pioneer Mill, Tel., 661-3129 for permit.

Hiking Distance & Time: 0.6 mile, 1/2 hour.

Driving Instructions:

From Lahaina (6 miles, 1/4 hour) southeast

on Route 30 to Olowalu Store.

From Wailuku (15 miles, 1/2 hour) south on Route 30 to Olowalu Store.

Introductory Notes: The Olowalu (lit., "many hills") Stream and shoreline is reported to be the best location on the island to find Maui diamonds (white quartz stones). These can be cut, polished, and set in rings and pendants. For the best results, they should be cut by a diamond cutter.

On the Trail: Walk behind the store to a water tank on the left and follow the sugar cane road that goes straight into the valley. The hike is

Graffitti - Hawaiian style

easy but warm through the cane fields. You may
see a variety of sugar cane operations. The cane
cycle includes planting, growth, irrigation, pest
control, tasseling (removing blossoms), burning
off (torching the field to burn away dead growth,
weeds and leaves), and harvesting over a period
of 18-21 months. Interesting, it requires one ton
of water to produce one pound of sugar!

You cannot miss the petroglyphs. They begin about 25 feet above the road on the face of a
rock outcropping. The remains of a viewing plat-
form enable you to locate the site. The
petroglyphs, several hundred years old, are
thought to have been carved by travelers passing through the mountains. The outcropping
provided a shady rest spot for weary hikers.
Unfortunately, some of the pictures have been
marred recently with spray paint. You can identify human figures, animals and boats. The human figures with large chests are thought to be
warriors or chiefs, while the stick figures are
probably commoners. Several figures in a row
or connected are probably members of one family. No one is allowed to hike beyond the
petroglyphs, since Olowalu Stream is a source
of drinking water.

LAHAINA TOWN
(Hiking Area No. 25)

(I have not provided a definitive narrative nor a map below of a hike/walk around Lahaina Town because the Honolulu Publishing Company, Ltd. has published a fine, free booklet, *Lahaina Historical Guide*, that contains a map of Lahaina containing a listing of 31 historical sites. Each site is conspicuously posted. The booklet is available at hotels, condominiums, restaurants, street corners and even at all those T-shirt shops. I have excerpted some highlights from their publication with their permission).

Zone: West.
Rating: Family.
Features: Historic walk through an old whaling town, through the former capitol of the Islands, and through the tourist center of Maui.
Permission: None.
Hiking Distance & Time: 1-3 miles, 1-3 hours.
Driving Instructions:
From Wailuku (21 miles, 1 hour) south on Route 30 to Front St.

Introductory Notes: Why hike Lahaina Town? Most who travel to Maui visit Lahaina. Anyone who visits Lahaina walks around Front Street. And anyone who walks Front Street should hike historic Lahaina. It's a marvelous way to spend the better part of a day and to learn more about Lahaina, Maui and Hawaii.

Lahaina is my kind of town. Oh sure, it's too touristy, it's overdeveloped and it has 50 more T-shirt shops than it needs, but I love it. I love the locals. I love the tourists. I love the strange people who urge sinners to repent and who hawk free trips that are never really free. And I love the gals checking out the guys and vice-versa. If you sit on Lahaina's sea wall for one hour after 8 p.m., every type of person in the world will pass by.

Lahaina was the capital of the Kingdom of Hawaii until 1860 when the capital city was moved to Honolulu. It also was an important whaling town and, consequently, a sailor's town for many years which gave it a "hot" reputation. Yes, I love Lahaina, and the best way to see it is by walking.

Plan a full day if you expect to visit all of the sites listed. I suggest you begin your outing at the Pioneer Inn (Site No. 8 in the booklet), where you can enjoy a hearty whaler's breakfast before starting out. It's obviously not important to hike/ walk in numerical order.

On the Trail: <u>Begin by finding a free copy of the *Lahaina Historical Guide* that contains a map and a listing of 31 historical sites.</u> I won't catalog all of the sites here, just a few of my favorite spots.

(REPRINTED BY PERMISSION of the HONO-
LULU PUBLISHING COMPANY, Ltd.)

Site #2, Baldwin Home (across from the library)

The missionary and Harvard trained physician Rev. Dwight Baldwin of Durham, Connecti-
cut, and his bride of a few weeks sailed from New
England for Hawaii in 1830. After first serving
in Waimea, he was assigned as pastor of
Lahaina's old Wainee Church. The Baldwins
moved into their home in 1838 and lived there
until 1871.

Built in 1834, the Baldwin home is the oldest standing building in Lahaina. It was built
with thick walls of coral, stone and hand-hewn
timbers. The addition of a bedroom and study in
1840 and a second story in 1849 accommodated
six children.

The Baldwin home served as a medical office
and as a center for missionary activity. Dr.
Baldwin received members of the royal court,
ships' captains, consuls and weary travelers. The
home has been faithfully restored by the Lahaina
Restoration Foundation and is open daily as a
museum. It presents a vivid picture of the life of
a missionary, physician and community force.

Site #7, Carthaginian (in the harbor)

The Carthaginian is a replica of a 19th-cen-
tury brig, typical of the small, fast freighters that

brought the first commerce to these Islands, and is the only authentically restored brig in the world.

The first Carthaginian was lost at sea in April, 1972 while on the way to Honolulu for drydock — a keen loss to the community. A replacement was finally found in Northern Europe, and a great dream was realized when the new Carthaginian crossed the seas with an all-Lahaina crew to her new home port. The sight of this majestic ship silhouetted against the sky is a sentimental reminder of Lahaina's heritage and the romance of the sea.

The Carthaginian features an exhibit on whales and whaling, with audio-visual displays, and an original whale boat that was discovered in Alaska and brought to Lahaina in 1973. The exhibit is open daily 9 a.m. to 4:30 p.m.

Site #8, Pioneer Inn (harbor front)

A dedicated member of the Royal Canadian Mounted Police, George Freeland, tracked a notorious criminal to Lahaina. Freeland fell in love with Lahaina and built the Pioneer Hotel in 1901 — for many years the only hotel in town. His family still owns the property.

Lahaina wasn't a major tourist center in the early days of the Pioneer Hotel, so Freeland built a service station and a movie theater to attract business. Pioneer Theatre became a major attraction. Benches were provided for the general public and reserved chairs were held for the privileged Pioneer Mill lunas (bosses).

Renovations and expansion of the Pioneer Hotel were completed in 1964. The bar and dining rooms feature an impressive collection of whaling artifacts and other salty memorabilia. It has a cozy little bar full of rowdy residents and visitors who bring back memories of Lahaina's whalers.

Site #9 Banyan Tree (east of the Pioneer Inn).

The banyan tree (Ficus benghalensis) came to Lahaina from India when it was only 8 feet tall. William O. Smith was Maui sheriff when he planted it in 1873 at a service marking the 50th anniversary of the founding of Lahaina's first Christian mission.

As the little town that was once the capital of the Hawaiian kingdom and the whaling capital of the world developed, the little tree grew — and grew. It provided a leisurely setting where local sugar mill employees and pineapple workers could meet and conduct business. It was also the scene of many a political rally, luau, dance, concert, festival and celebration. For years it shaded viewers at the elementary school's May Day festivities, whaling sprees and Aloha Week observances. Some residents still recall swinging Tarzan-like on the aerial roots (and being swatted with a rake by the caretaker).

Lahaina's banyan now has 12 major trunks

of varying girth, besides the huge core of central trunks. It reaches upward to a height of about 50 feet and stretches outward over a 200-foot area, shading two-thirds of an acre on the almost 2 acres of land in the courthouse square.

Site #21, The Old Prison (Wainee and Prison Streets)

On the corner of Wainee and Prison streets is a building known as "The prison." Hale Paahao, "the stuck-in-irons house," was so named because of its standard wall shackles and ball-and-chain restraints.

Before the prison was built, sailors who ignored the warning of the Hawaiian soldiers to return to their ships at sunset were kept overnight in the fort (Site 11) It has a reputation for being a very uncomfortable place to spend the night.

In 1851 the fort physician recommended that prisoners not sleep on the ground; it made them ill, and sick prisoners were a liability to the government. So the Kingdom of Hawaii decided to build a larger facility to serve Maui, Molokai and Lanai. Convict laborers stripped the coral block from the fort and used it to construct the compound. The prison house was built of planks in 1852; it had separate quarters for men and women.

A guard patrolled the grounds from a catwalk. Most prisoners were there for deserting ship, drunkenness, working on the Sabbath or reckless horse riding. Those jailed for longer than a year were sent to Oahu.

Site #31, Jodo Mission (Mala Wharf)

The Lahaina Jodo Mission Cultural Park sits on a point of land known as Puunoa Point, "the hill freed from taboo." The area was once a small village fronting the royal grove of coconut trees planted by the governor of Maui's wife, Hoapiliwahine. The area was called Mala ("garden") and the adjacent Mala Wharf still bears the name. The park was a pleasant place to the many Japanese laborers who stamped it with their own cultural heritage.

The mission is the best known landmark in the area today and is one of Lahaina's busiest visitor attractions. The largest Buddha outside of Japan sits majestically and serenely in a small park commemorating the arrival of the first Japanese immigrants in 1968. The compound includes the temple shrine and an extensive outdoor meeting area.

Members of the church are very active in the community, and many outside functions, such as wedding receptions and award ceremonies, are frequently held here. As with many other Buddhist temples, the Jodo Mission celebrates the summer Bon Memorial Celebration, joyous drum-dancing festival honoring ancestral souls.

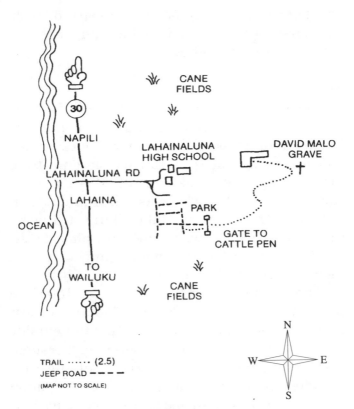

TRAIL ····· (2.5)
JEEP ROAD − − − −
(MAP NOT TO SCALE)

LAHAINA "L"
(Hiking Area No. 26)

Zone: West.
Rating: Strenous.
Features: Views of the west side, Lanai, Molokai, David Malo's grave.
Permission: Pioneer Mill Co., Ldt. Tel., 661-3129 for permit.

Hiking Distance & Time: 2.5 miles, 2 hours, 1,000-foot gain.

Driving Instructions:

From Lahaina, drive to Lahainaluna Road to the Pioneer Mill Co. office. Drive up Lahainaluna Road to where it turns right go past the football field and park outside the gate that crosses the cane road.

From Wailuku (21 miles, 1 hour) south on Route 30 to Lahainaluna Road, then as above.

Introductory Notes: The Lahaina "L" is a familiar spot to visitors and a popular hike for local people. The 30-foot limestone "L" engraved on the mountainside is maintained by students at Lahainaluna High School, who make periodic trips to apply fresh coats of lime. On graduation day each year, torch-bearing students create a spectacular display by illuminating the "L".

Students also yearly make the hike to David Malo's gravesite a few hundred feet above the "L" to clean the area and to place a commemorative plaque in cement. David Malo was a local Hawaiian hero who worked for the well-being of his people in education and economics. He introduced cotton planting and sought to have the people grow sugar. He believed that the people should own the land. Malo was born in North Kona, but moved to Maui and became, in 1831, one of the first students at Lahainaluna High School, at the age of 38. During his lifetime, he

wrote an early history of the Sandwich Islands
called *Hawaiian Antiquities*; he became a poet
of some reputation; and he was the Commis-
sioner of Education for Molokai, Lanai and Maui.
Annually, pageants are held on Maui commemorating his life and contributions.

On the Trail: If you have a jeep or a four-
wheeled drive vehicle the Pioneer Mill Co. will
probably allow you to drive on the cane road to a
cattle pen shaded by large eucalyptus trees,
which is to the right and below the "L". If not,
you should be allowed to drive to a row of mango
trees just below the cattle pen and then hike up
to it.

From the cattle pen, the "L" is up the mountain to the left, although you cannot see it from
here. Lahaina lies below, with the island of Lanai
directly offshore and the island of Molokai to the
northwest. Climb over the fence into the pen
and pick up a foot trail on the far left side.

There is a trail of sorts through the pasture
land heading up the mountain, bearing to the
left. Follow the rain cuts in the earth so that
you are making a partial loop in the direction of
the Malo gravesite, about 200 feet above the "L."
Low scrub dominates the area, accentuated by
multicolored lantana (Lantana camara), which
is common in the lower, more arid portions of
the island.

From the Malo gravesite it is a short hike

down to the "L."

Return and visit the high school, which is the oldest American school west of the Rockies, having opened its doors in 1831. It also has a small museum which houses the first printing press on the islands. It is open to the public.

Rare Pu'e (Bog Lobelia) - West Maui Mts.

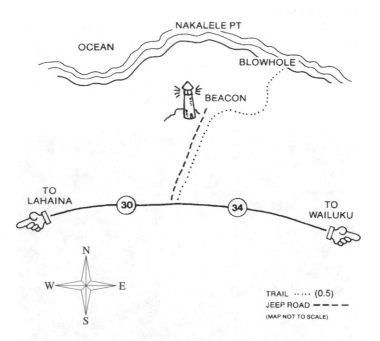

NAKALELE BLOWHOLE
(Hiking Area No. 27)

Zone: West.
Rating: Family.
Features: Blowhole, tide pools, lava formations, crashing surf.
Permission: None.
Hiking Distance & Time: 0.5 mile, 1/2 hour.
Driving Instructions:

From Lahaina (18 miles, 3/4 hour) north on Route 30, which becomes Route 34 after Honokahau, to Coast Guard beacon.

From Wailuku (39 miles, 1 1/2 hours) south on Route 30, which becomes Route 34 after Honokahau, to Coast Guard beacon.

Introductory Notes: Nakalele (lit., "the leaning") Blowhole is fun for the family and provides a restful and serene escape.

On the Trail: Take the jeep trail to the bluff overlooking the Coast Guard beacon and blowhole. From here, it is a walk of a few hundred yards to the blowhole. Part of the fun is trying to locate the blowhole. Do not expect to find any signs or arrows. If you choose to walk out to the blowhole, USE EXTREME CAUTION, for the footing is uncertain and the swells are unpredictable. You will probably get sprayed as the surf crashes against the rocks before you sight the blowhole.

Everyone will enjoy the tide pools, which contain an abundant sampling of sea life. Ask the children to give fanciful names to the interesting lava configurations caused by the ocean's rapid cooling of the once-molten flow.

APPENDIX

(Write to)
Superintendent
Haleakala National Park
P.O. Box 369
Makawao, Maui, HI 96768

+ park information
+ crater cabin reservations

(In person)
Haleakala National Park HQ
Crater Road
(808) 572-9306

+ park information
+ crater camping permit
+ crater cabin keys

Division of State Parks
54 So High St. Room 101
Wailuku, Maui, HI 96793
(808) 984-8109

+ camping permits
  for state parks
+ cabin rental reservations
  for state parks

Dep't of Parks & Rec.
War Memorial Gym
1580 Kaahumanu Ave.
Wailuku, Maui, HI 96793
(808) 243-7389

+ camping permits for
  county campgrounds

Division of Forestry
54 So High St Room 101
Wailuku, Maui, HI 96793
 (808) 984-8100

**+ hiking permission for
Kanaha Bird Sanctuary**

Maui Visitors Bureau
P.O. Box 1738
Kahului, Maui, HI 96732
(808) 244-3530

+ general tourist info

Maui Pineapple Co.
4900 Honoapiilani Hwy
Lahaina, Maui, HI 96761
(808) 669-6201

**+ camping at
Windmill Beach**

Camp Pecusa
800 Olowalu Village
Lahaina, Maui, HI 96761
(808) 661-4303

**+ camping and
cabin reservations**

INDEX

TRAIL NOTES

TRAIL NOTES

TRAIL NOTES

OUR NEW VIDEO:
"HAWAII ON FOOT"
See Hawaii as few have with

ROBERT SMITH

For his video, *HAWAII ON FOOT*, Smith has taken some of the best dayhikes and backpacks on the four major islands from his books to give the viewer a sampling of the best trails on Maui, Hawaii, Oahu and Kauai.

Here are hikes in Haleakala and Hawaii Volcanoes National Parks, backpacks deep into the Kauai wilderness, strolls into Maui's verdant valleys and walks along the black sand beaches of Hawaii.

There are hikes for the dayhiker and the backpacker, for the novice and the experienced outdoorsperson, and for children and their grandparents.

HAWAII ON FOOT also contains camping and state rental housekeeping cabin information – Hawaii's best bargain – and tips on hiking and backpacking equipment.

ORDER FORM

HIKING KAUAI	$10.95
HIKING MAUI	$10.95
HIKING HAWAII	$10.95
HAWAII'S BEST HIKING TRAILS	$15.95
VIDEO: HAWAII ON FOOT	$12.95

FORWARD TO:

NAME: _____

ADDRESS: _____

CITY: _____ STATE: ____ ZIP: _____

QUANTITY		PRICE		TOTAL
____ HIKING KAUAI	@	$10.95	=	
____ HIKING MAUI	@	$10.95	=	
____ HIKING HAWAII	@	$10.95	=	
____ HAWAII'S BEST HIKING TRAILS	@	$15.95	=	
____ VIDEO: HAWAII ON FOOT	@	$12.95	=	
	Postage/Handling (1st Class)		=	$3.20

TOTAL ENCLOSED = _____

MAIL TO:
Hawaiian Outdoor Adventures Publications
102-16 Kaui Place
Kula, Maui, HI 96790
TEL/FAX (808) 878-2664
E-MAIL>hionfoot@maui.net
WEBPAGE>http://www.maui.net/~hionfoot